PRAYER THAT
MOVES
MOUNTAINS

DIANE PESTES

Pacific Press®
Publishing Association
Nampa, Idaho | Oshawa, Ontario, Canada
www.pacificpress.com

Cover design by Gerald Lee Monks
Cover design resources from iStockphoto.com
Interior design by Aaron Troia

The author assumes full responsibility for the accuracy of all facts and quotations as cited in this book.

You can obtain additional copies of this book by calling toll-free 1-800-765-6955 or by visiting http://www.adventistbookcenter.com.

Library of Congress Cataloging-in-Publication Data:
Pestes, Diane, 1964-
  Prayer that moves mountains / Diane Pestes.
     pages cm
  Includes bibliographical references.
  ISBN 978-0-8163-5895-3 (pbk.)
  1. Prayer—Christianity. I. Title.
  BV210.3.P453 2016
  248.3'2—dc23
                                      2015035433

January 2016

To my heavenly Father:

Thank You for dying to save me and showing me that I can make a difference too. I look forward to all of eternity with You and Your people.

Acknowledgments

Special thanks to the following:

My parents, Marion and Ruthanne Bixel, for their prayers and love for me before I was even born; for believing any risk would be worth it; and for their faithful, dedicated, and tireless examples of service to God in their daily lives.

My husband, Ron Pestes, for his love and support and sharing our many interesting life adventures.

My prayer partners—Lois Meythaler, Corleen Johnson, Linda Lydick, and Georgia Shaffer. Thanks for your many prayers, friendship, and the amazing stories of lives we have touched for eternity.

Ione Richardson and Tawny Sportsman for their prayers, friendship, and advice.

Without all of these people mentioned, and family and friends too numerous to mention, there would not be incredible, faith-building, life-changing, inspirational, and encouraging stories of how God can transform lives and add to the population of heaven.

Contents

Does God Involve Himself in Our Lives?

"For I know the plans I have for you," declares the LORD, *"plans to prosper you and not to harm you, plans to give you hope and a future."*
—*Jeremiah 29:11*

At the beginning of a year, many people make resolutions and projections about what the new year will bring. One Sabbath afternoon in December, while walking with my friend Sandy, she asked me, "What are you going to do in the new year?"

"I'm going to write a book called *Prayer That Moves Mountains,* a collection of stories about 'God moments' that happen to people," I replied. Switching topics, I asked, "Do you know of a free place with festive Christmas lights to view tonight?"

"Yes, there is a place called Celebration of Lights about twenty-five minutes away. I'll go with you if you decide to go," Sandy enthused.

Soon my husband Ron, Sandy, and I found ourselves enjoying a twenty-year family tradition in honor of their daughter's December 8 birthday. Every year the celebration becomes larger. We were delighted to experience at least twenty different lighted areas, Nativity displays, ponds, gazebos with Christmas trees and gas fireplaces, and a huge walk-in snow globe depicting how several countries around the world celebrate Christmas. A lodge prepared for relaxing and complete with free cookies, hot chocolate, and apple cider was also there. In the far corner of the lodge, there were comfortable chairs near a gas fireplace. Drawn in like a thirsty person to water, I beckoned to Ron and Sandy, "Let's sit over there awhile."

At least twenty minutes went by before a man walked up and asked, "Are you from the church?"

Ron responded, "We are from a church. Which one did you mean?"

The man did not answer the question but stepped in closer and expressed sadly, "My mother has been in the hospital for two and a half months, and she needs prayer."

Ron instantly urged, "Well, Diane prays for people."

I leaned over to Ron and suggested, "Could you move over so this man can sit down?" I intended for the man to sit by me, so I could ask a few more questions. Ron missed the cue, jumped up, and the man apparently thought we were standing to pray and took Ron's hand. Sandy, as if in unison, stood up and took the man's other hand. Sensing this was not a moment to chat, I stood up, grasped Ron's and Sandy's hands, and asked, "What's your mother's name?"

"Marnie," he replied.

I lifted up a prayer to God for Marnie and peace for this man. When I finished, he thanked us and walked away. We sat down, and Sandy exclaimed, "Well, Diane, there's a story for your book!"

Sometimes, from our limited perspective, it seems God has not intervened in a special way. When I look back over what God has done in the past year, or the past several, I am truly amazed at how many times it was obvious that God was involved. I mean really involved! Sometimes small, sometimes big, each one makes me realize, "I'm thrilled that God really is interested in me personally." Not only does God want to get our attention and intervene in ways that bless our lives, but He also can reach others through us. He loves making connection moments happen.

Thriving versus surviving

Joseph is my favorite Bible hero because of the way he found and maintained his sole identity in God through loss, false accusations, and adversity. He stood up for the right, and God honored and used his honest life to bless and save others. Genesis 39:23 states, "The Lord was with him and caused everything he did to succeed" (NLT). This gives evidence that God was intervening in his life. Thankfully, Moses records Joseph's entire story for us to follow. If we were to stop reading his story in the middle, we might become depressed. But, by the end, it becomes an amazing story of loose ends recovered.

"Although God loves us, believing and obeying Him do not shelter us from life's calamities. Setbacks, tragedies, and sorrows strike Christians and non-Christians alike. But in our tests and trials, God expects us to express our faith to the world. How do you respond to your troubles? Do you ask God, 'Why me?' or do you say, 'Use me!' "[1]

It seems, at times, that God "forces" us to go through hard things only to find out later that we use those God-moment stories as powerful illustrations of His love and grace. The first seven weeks of my life were spent in foster care while a custody battle ensued. The court system asserted that my adoptive parents could not afford a surgery I would need later. Meanwhile, my adoptive parents spent that time in constant prayer. Knowing this has permanently instilled in me the bigger picture of God and the devil fighting over us.

Several years of my life were spent in the credit union industry marketing their wonderful motto, "People helping people." Yet, in the back of my mind, I longed for something more "missionlike." As a child, I was fascinated by stories of missionaries. The stories in *Prayer That Moves Mountains* show that God works through ordinary people to be missionaries, wherever they are, and sometimes He even adds in a few miraculous moments.

Our inestimable worth

Consider my advice: start a journal to record when God intervenes in your life. Jeremiah 29:11 says, " 'For I know the plans I have for you,' declares the LORD, 'plans to prosper you and not to harm you, plans to give you hope and a future.' " This book describes how God weaves different people in and out of our lives to shape, encourage, and change us. It also shows how God personally speaks, delights, blesses, and provides joy in our work for Him. Let us continue on this journey of stories and helpful insights I have learned along the way. At the end of each chapter, there will be a few "Moments of Reflection" questions that you can use for personal introspection or with a group.

Let us pray as we begin, "Heavenly Father, we adore You, and we praise You because of Your gift of Jesus on the cross, so that we might have eternal life. You are our strength, our joy, and our salvation. Please forgive us for doubting Your goodness. Thank You for Your forgiveness, for You say, 'If we confess our sins, he is faithful and just and will forgive us our sins and purify us from all unrighteousness' (1 John 1:9). We do not want to say, 'Why me?' when trouble befalls us; instead, teach us to say, 'Use me,' because You restore our lives to bless others. For every person reading this book, I ask that You will refresh them, encourage them, restore them, and pour out Your Holy Spirit upon them. Bring us all into Your soon-coming kingdom. We thank You for Your love and involvement. We thank You for Your Holy Spirit and what You will do because we ask, in Jesus' name, amen!"

---

1. *Life Application Study Bible: New Living Translation* (Wheaton, IL: Tyndale House Publishers, 2004), 784.

CHAPTER ONE

One Choice Can Change a Life

In their hearts humans plan their course,
but the LORD *establishes their steps.*

—*Proverbs 16:9*

Have you ever taken a vacation and come back more frazzled than before you left? My husband, Ron, and I always wanted to go to Europe. So, along with my parents, we decided to visit eight countries in seventeen days on a tour bus to minimize worries about meals, hotels, rental cars, and so on. After a long day on the way to Vienna, Ron and I decided we were tired of touring by bus. My parents seemed unfazed by the ride and wished for a walk around the hotel for some sightseeing. We gathered our luggage, waited for forty people to check in, and trudged up five flights of stairs. "I have a headache," Ron said. "Let's not walk around the city but rest for a while."

"That's a good idea. I'm tired too," I replied. I put a few items away and lay on the bed. Soon after, the fire alarm went off. Ron jumped up and sprinted for the door before he realized I was not following. He turned back to me. "Aren't you coming?"

"No," I said.

"What?" he replied with a shocked look, adding, "The building may be on fire. We have to leave."

"I don't feel compelled," I replied and did not budge.

My husband of five years looked like he was weighing the full measure of his life at that moment. He pleaded, "But we have barely begun life together, and I want to spend more time with you. I don't want to leave you."

"I'm staying," I said. "I don't feel compelled to leave."

"But the building may be on fire! If I leave, I may never see you again!"

To which I replied, "I hope you have a nice life."

Sounds cold, doesn't it? That happened when I was in my twenties. I was convinced I was not going to waste my energy by running downstairs when I was certain I did not need to.

Ron looked at the door, then at me as he quickly processed this information in his head: life or wife, life or wife, life or wife. Life eventually won out; he took one last look at me and left.

Twenty minutes later Ron returned, looking frazzled. "There really was a fire," he said. "It was in the kitchen, and I watched as people ran around and finally put it out." What if the fire had really gotten out of control? What makes one person heed the warning signs, while another totally ignores them?

When I think about choices, consequences, and God's response in the Bible, I see a message of grace that far outweighs the warnings. If I were to describe the whole Bible in three words, I would say, "God is love." If I were to describe it in one sentence, I would use 1 Kings 18:21: "How long will you waver between two opinions? If the LORD is God, follow him; but if Baal is God, follow him." In other words, do you want the God of love or the enemy resolved to destroy? God loves each of us unconditionally and demonstrates that He is actively involved in our lives.

When I was in college, the transit system ran a special: With just ten cents and a student card, you could ride the bus one way into town. Often I did not even have that much.

One day the college sent me a letter, stating, "You need to pay two thousand dollars, or else you will not be able to register for next quarter." Have you ever received a letter to cough up money or else? I worked in credit unions before college, and I had seen vehicles repossessed. So when I received my college letter, I was desperate and fell to the floor before God to plead and pray. "Heavenly Father, I need Your help! My parents and grandparents are all tapped out. I don't have any money. You are all I have. You see the letter I received and can get me in next quarter. Only You can solve this." A half hour later, I got up and headed over to see the finance person. "I just don't have anything for next quarter," I said.

She replied, "Would you believe that right before you came in, I received a phone call from someone that will donate two thousand dollars? You can have it. All they want is a thank-you note." She pushed paper and a pen across the desk to me. Awestruck, I took the pen and wrote a heartfelt thank-you note. That is amazing grace! My desperation drove me to prayer, and God responded to my cry for help.

14

God speaks to individuals

Jonah received a warning message from the Lord, stating, "Go to the great city of Nineveh and preach against it, because its wickedness has come up before me" (Jonah 1:2). Jonah finally went, after spending three days in the belly of a big fish, saying a prayer of distress and receiving the message a second time.

What did the Ninevites do? They repented, fasted, and prayed. Even the king covered himself with sackcloth and ashes. Jonah 4:2 says that God relented from sending calamity. Everyone that turns to God is His favorite, but, even then, we do not always receive instant results. Instead, there are many verses that encourage us along our journey through life: Jeremiah 29:11; Proverbs 3:5, 6; and this one, which I really like, in Proverbs 16:9, "In their hearts humans plan their course, but the LORD establishes their steps." This verse is easier to understand and accept when we look in hindsight; when looking forward, it is easy to become discouraged. In fact, sometimes God's involvement takes several years to unfold.

During my senior year at a Christian academy, my friend Jennifer asked me to go with her to an upcoming regional Christian Bible conference. The conference was not in an exciting location nor did it sound like fun. So I responded, "No, I do not want to go."

Jennifer replied, "But maybe God wants you to do this. You should pray about it."

How could I answer that without praying? So I spent a few days in prayer and was surprised to find God saying, "Go!" Oddly enough, Jennifer got sick a few days before the event and was not able to attend. Since I knew God had said, "Go," I went by myself. On Friday evening, there was a get-together in a large hall. I walked in, headed clear across to the other side of the building, and sat in the back where I could view the whole crowd. *Hmm, I feel a little awkward sitting by myself without a friend. Lord, show me why I'm here.* Just then two teens walked in the door. These girls appeared to be head and shoulders above the crowd. Just as I thought, *They are really tall. I wonder how tall they are,* God said to me, *"Pray that they will be your friends."*

What? Is God kidding? I don't even know these people. They don't go to my school. Very curious about how God could get these tall people to be my friends and knowing God said it would take prayer, I started praying about it.

Praying about something you cannot see takes faith. The Bible says, "We live by faith, not by sight" (2 Corinthians 5:7). This was the fall of my senior year, and I continued to pray about it for a few months. After that, I did not think about it much. Imagine my surprise when I saw the two tall girls in my summer college English class and also sunbathing on the roof while listening to loud rock music. Except for small chit-chat that whole summer, we did not become fast friends. So I resumed praying.

Summer turned into the fall quarter, and out of hundreds of room com-binations it seemed to be divinely directed that the tall girls moved in next door. I went over to say hello. They were nice enough; and in the days that followed, I kept making excuses to visit. Teri gave me a hot chocolate and coffee drink every time I came over. It tasted good, so I kept going back, all the while remembering God's words in my head, *"Pray that they will be your friends."* I wondered just what God was going to do with this story. One time curiosity got the best of me, and I asked, "Jackie and Teri, how tall are you?"

"We get that question all the time," Jackie said. "I'm five feet nine, and Teri is five feet eleven."

They drove my roommate absolutely crazy. Bonnie* was into Christian music and thought the tall girls were to be avoided at all costs. I do not know how many times she warned me to stay away because their loud rock music played right through the walls and, as she put it, "Surely these girls are evil. They even go to parties." But Bonnie had not heard God's voice in my head, and I was not about to tell anyone what God had said. So I just kept visiting Jackie and Teri. By the end of first quarter, though, Teri had grown weary of college, probably because of too much time spent partying and not enough time spent on classes, so she moved back home. I was sad that my prayers for her to stop partying did not seem to be answered. Bonnie continued to be horrified and finally said, "I am moving out because you have the wrong type of friends." Looking back, it is easy to see that this was divine involvement. Jackie and I were without roommates, so we decided to room together and, yes, we became good friends.

One choice makes a difference

Little did I know then how this academy prayer was going to affect the rest of my life. After my sophomore year, Jackie and her boyfriend Kevin moved to another location, where Kevin would be taking nurse's training. *Hmm, Lord, who should be my next roommate?* I prayed about it and then

---

* Bonnie is a pseudonym.

called the dean. "There is a woman named Lois you should go visit," she said, giving me a phone number. "She needs a roommate next year."

We spoke over the phone, and I asked to visit her. Lois was into classical music, and I was listening to rock music and some Christian stuff (a big deal when sharing a small room). However, we both liked to pray. Sometimes we would talk about what worked with prayer and what did not. Other times we would pray about our future husbands.

At the end of our first year as roommates, Lois shared that she was going away to be a student missionary for a year.

The last day of school as I was saying Goodbye to Lois, God whispered to me, *"She's going to be your prayer partner fourteen years from now."*

What? I shuddered. *I can't even imagine what I'll be doing fourteen years from now.* Sometimes it is difficult to grasp how some of God's statements tie into the future.

Late in my senior year of college, I received a call from Jackie. "I'm getting married, and I want you to be a bridesmaid," she said.

"I would be honored to be one," I replied excitedly.

"It's going to be two days after your graduation, so it won't interrupt school for you or my fiancé, Kevin," she said. What an answer to that prayer at the Bible conference in academy! Now I would be a bridesmaid!

The rest of the year flew by, and my parents came up for my graduation. Out on the lawn after the ceremonies, while everyone was being congratulated, my mother said to me, "Since you did not find a man in college, he will be even harder to find." And she went on to share some statistics. I was startled by her words (she later said she was joking), but I had a quick comeback: "Mother, God knows just exactly where my man is; and when the timing is right, we will meet."

Two days later I was a bridesmaid in Jackie and Kevin's lovely wedding. Later, at the reception, people were chatting and eating cake. Usually, I look for someone to talk with, but I started to feel uncomfortable, as if I was not supposed to be where I was. To shake the feeling, I decided to go outside for a few minutes. As I exited the building, I saw a lone man with a video camera. The night before, at the rehearsal, he had said hello to me, but I did not know his name.

Now, at the reception, I was prepared as I said, "Hey, Ron, is that your video camera?"

At our wedding one year and four months later, we shared the story of my mom's words after my college graduation. Of course, Jackie and Lois were bridesmaids, and Kevin was a groomsman. That was about four and a half years after I prayed that the tall girls would be my friends.

God wants to be first in our lives in everything. He is eager for us to trust Him with all the details. Trusting Him now and each day that comes will help to develop a pattern for trust when an emergency decision arises. My husband and I are extremely grateful that I made the right choice about going to the Bible conference and then prayed when God asked me to. Sometimes an earthly choice can make an eternal difference.

Sometimes one choice can save another

One April day I went to my mother's house to care for my father while she took a break. However, as I sat at the kitchen table, I realized I was too tired to help. *How long have I felt like this? I feel a little strange. I should go home and lie down.* Thirty minutes later, while lying down, I realized my heart was beating irregularly. *I'm so busy and must have been in denial. I think this has been going on for a while. This is not good.* I called a paramedic friend. "Lewie, I have lost all my energy, and my heart is beating double beats."

"Go to the emergency room," he said.

"I don't want to go to the emergency room. Are you sure this isn't just one of those menstrual times women get?"

"You don't want to play with your heart. You need to go to the emergency room."

I thought, *Well, that was not very fun advice. I need a second opinion.* After all, who wants to go to the emergency room? I have gone before with my mother to the emergency room, and they usually admitted her—sometimes for days at a time. *This could disrupt my whole week,* I thought. So I called my regular doctor's after-hours number. His advice? "Go to the emergency room now!"

Oh, good grief, there's no way around this one.

"Ron, we need to go to the emergency room," I said as I stood up, walked into the kitchen, and grabbed my purse. This was news to him because I had not shared my warning signs with him. While Ron drove, I notified four close friends, asking for prayer.

If you mention the word *heart,* they call you right in for an electrocardiogram (EKG). However, they kept sending me out to the waiting room because they did not have a room for me. All twenty-five emergency rooms were full. Between tests, they sent me out to the waiting room. Ron was pacing back and forth. Several hours went by, and I finally sent him to Taco Bell for food. *Good grief, it feels like I'm by myself,* I thought. Except that I was holding on to God's hand, "For I am the LORD your God who takes hold of your right hand and says to you, Do not fear; I will help you" (Isaiah 41:13).

While Ron was away, a man came in, stood in front of me, and asked, "Is someone sitting beside you?"

"No," I responded. Even though there were plenty of seats, he sat down one seat from me. Then he grabbed his side, doubled over, and loudly moaned.

I leaned in toward him and asked, "Are you in pain?"

"I was debating whether to kill myself or come here," he sighed.

Instantly, I knew I had chosen wisely to come to the emergency room. Good thing we both finally heeded the warning signs. It is interesting that in order to reach someone in an emergency situation, I had to be in an emergency situation myself.

The man, whose name was Richard, and I had a good hour-long conversation. At the end, when they finally called his name, he said, "You have been an angel. I don't know what I would have done without you. You kept me calm and gave me hope." Praise the Lord the emergency room beds were full, I made a good choice, and God was involved. "In their hearts humans plan their course, but the LORD establishes their steps" (Proverbs 16:9).

Moments of Reflection:

1. Read Revelation 1:1–8 for the rest of the story of how God will rescue us from this world's emergency situation.

2. Have you ever felt impressed to pray about someone or something? Did you note the date and circumstances in your journal and begin to pray about it? If you did, lift up a prayer of praise to God for looking out for you. If you did not, plan to do so the next time.

3. Jot down any emotions you may feel about similar circumstances to those mentioned here. Also jot down any Scripture promises you find to claim for yourself.

4. If you have been impressed to pray about someone or something and you have seen at least a partial answer, write it down or share your testimony with your group.

CHAPTER TWO

When You Least Expect It!

Being confident of this, that he who began a good work in you
will carry it on to completion until the day of Christ Jesus.
—Philippians 1:6

O ne night, during my childhood, I turned on my little lamp, pulled back the bedcovers, got in, and looked up at the ceiling. What! There was a spider on the ceiling above me. *I can't sleep with a bug crawling around above me,* I thought. It was too high for me to reach, and I did not want to touch the spider anyway, so I started shouting, "Mother, Mother, Mother!" Soon she came in. I pointed at the ceiling and said, "Could you get that spider?" She went out the door to get a tissue and came back and stood on the bed. Assuming she would be successful, I did not get out of the bed. She reached as high as she could, made a grab at the spider, missed, then said, "Uh-oh, oops." I looked up. No spider. *If she didn't get it, then it must have dropped straight down on to the bed!*

My mother said, "Oh well. Go to sleep now, dear."

Yeah, right! I bolted out of bed, peered at the covers, lifted each one carefully, and looked intently. My frantic search was in vain—the spider was nowhere to be found. My mother left the room certain that I would be content. Do you think I slept soundly? No!

Staying awake

If I told you Jesus Christ were coming today, would you believe me? No, you would shake your head and recite Matthew 25:13: "So, you too, must keep watch! For you do not know the day or hour of my return" (NLT). Or you might recite Revelation 16:15: "Look, I come like a thief! Blessed is the one who stays awake."

Many people look like they are spiritually asleep. However, God may not be finished with them yet. This fact should bring us great encouragement. Philippians 1:6 states, "Being confident of this, that he who began a good work in you will carry it on to completion until the day of Christ Jesus."

God's good work

One day while home from college for the summer, I was sitting in the backyard, listening to my favorite rock music station. Maybe you think God cannot deliver your son or daughter or you from distracting music messages. Think again! God interrupted my thoughts and started speaking to me. And it was not just a one-liner message. I jumped up and ran into the house for paper and pen and started writing. It was a message with a theme: "Incorporating God Into the Daily Life." I looked at the paper, and I thought, *Now what am I going to do with this message?* I kept the paper and wondered the rest of the summer.

My junior year of college began, and I forgot about the paper. One day Lois and I were sitting during the chapel service, listening to the devotional. When the speaker was done, a man made an announcement: "We are going to have a student Week of Prayer in January. If you are interested in speaking, give me a call." I felt God tugging at me, so I called the man a couple of days later. We met at a building near my dorm. "You are the only one to volunteer," he said. "It took many phone calls to get others to speak. What made you call me?"

"I have always loved the Lord since I was a small child, and I want to be obedient to what He says," I said. "And I felt God prompting me to speak."

He affirmed my decision. "I have five envelopes with five different topics. Do you want to know what the topics are or just choose an envelope?"

I replied, "God knows what they are and which one I need to use. Let's pray over them." We did, and then I said, "Mix them up, and I will choose." I reached for an envelope, opened it, and did a double-take as I read the words: "Incorporating God Into the Daily Life." *Incredible,* I thought. *I already have part of the talk written.*

My mother was a little shocked when I told her I would be speaking in the college church in front of more than a thousand people. She said, "I remember one time when you were little you stood on stage and opened your mouth, and nothing came out."

"Well, I'm not little anymore," I replied. A few months later, my parents came up to listen. My father, who was very proud and encouraging, took my hands for a moment of prayer over me in their motel room before I shared God's talk.

Just when you think, *So that's a great story and surely what God had in mind that summer day,* it gets better, because God's not finished "until the day of Christ Jesus." The very next day I was walking toward the women's dorm when the dean saw me. "I want to see you in my office," she said. "Can you come tomorrow?"

What can this mean? As I sat in her office the next day, the dean began with, "I heard your presentation and was personally blessed. Not many people are willing to be speakers, and that took a lot of confidence. I want to offer you a job. You can have any job in my power to give, and I have three in mind. I'm creating the new position of chaplain for the whole dorm. You would give worships three times a week and visit the sick and anyone else that needs visiting. Or you can be a resident assistant or the head resident assistant. Or you can be all three."

Head resident assistant meant that if she or the other dean were gone, I would be in charge. I liked that idea. So I said, "I'll be the head resident assistant and the chaplain."

Heart for people

Because I have a heart for people, it was exciting to be able to visit the sick, pray with them, and give three dorm worships each week. One of my best worship talks happened one night when I had not planned in advance. I was visiting someone at the complete opposite side of the dorm from the worship room when I suddenly remembered I was due to share worship. Startled, I glanced at my watch, noticed worship was starting in five minutes, thought, *Oh no, I didn't prepare anything,* and took off running as fast as I could go.

Lord, help! Lord, help me with the right worship talk, I prayed. Everyone was looking at me as I sat, breathing hard. God blessed, and a testimony about how He provides came out of my head. Word apparently got out because the next worship was packed.

God is able to give us words in an emergency when we ask. But there are times when we forget to ask; Joshua had one of those experiences. As referenced in the Bible, Joshua was a brilliant military leader and a strong spiritual influence. When Moses died, Joshua was put in charge of all the Israelites, and the key to his success was his submission to God. When God spoke, Joshua listened and obeyed.

As Hudson Taylor said, "God's work done in God's way" will bring success. The standard for success, however, is not set by the world around us, but by God's Word. Joshua was in the middle of destroying enemy people in the Promised Land, and those enemies were afraid. Joshua 9:3–7 records the following:

> When the people of Gibeon heard what Joshua had done to Jericho and Ai, they resorted to a ruse: They went as a delegation whose donkeys were loaded with worn-out sacks and old wineskins, cracked and mended. They put worn and patched sandals on their feet and wore old clothes. All the bread of their food supply was dry and moldy. Then they went to Joshua in the camp at Gilgal and said to him and the Israelites, "We have come from a distant country; make a treaty with us."
>
> The Israelites said to the Hivites, "But perhaps you live near us, so how can we make a treaty with you?"

These people were not interested in Joshua's God; they just wanted to protect their lives. In a moment of self-sufficiency, "The Israelites sampled their provisions but did not inquire of the LORD" (verse 14). They trusted their feelings. They trusted what they saw with their eyes—a big mistake.

Three days later they regretted their decision when they learned the Gibeonites were close neighbors. We can learn from Joshua's mistake that we should be alert and inquire of the Lord.

Divine intervention when least expected

One day Paula, the dean, called me to say, "The other dean and I are going to be away this evening. Could you come down and go over a few details?" It was to be my first time manning the dorm with both deans gone. Excited, I said a quick prayer: "Lord, please guide me and show me what I need to know," and ran down the six flights of stairs. We were talking over the details, and the dean was just about to leave when I suddenly had a nagging thought: *What if someone gets trapped in the elevator?* I asked, "What do I do if someone gets trapped in the elevator?"

"That never happens," Paula replied.

I responded, "Well, just in case it did, what would I do? Is there a button to push?"

We went downstairs to the ground floor, and she showed me something to reset. About an hour later, as I was sitting in "my office," I heard women screaming from inside the elevator. "We're stuck; we're stuck, help!"

Jumping up instantly, I thought, *Good thing I asked the question. God, You are so good!* I ran to the elevator and yelled up to the women, "Hold tight a moment! I have to run downstairs and reset a lever!" A moment later I ran upstairs just as the doors were opening on the second floor. The women leaped out of it, saying, "We thought we were going to be stuck forever; thank you." The nagging thought from earlier turned out to be God's provision in advance!

One exciting example in the Bible is found in Exodus 14. Everything was going well until the Israelites encountered the Red Sea in front of them with the Egyptians bearing down on them from behind. God had a plan in place, but the Israelites were unaware of it. God lovingly reminds us in Exodus 14:13, 14, "Do not be afraid. Stand firm and you will see the deliverance the LORD will bring you today. . . . The LORD will fight for you; you need only to be still." And we read that the Lord opened the sea for them to get out in a new direction. Sometimes, when you least expect it, God shows up with divine involvement and carries out His plan. "He who began a good work in you will carry it on to completion" (Philippians 1:6).

Moments of Reflection:

1. Have you ever felt stuck? What was the first thought to come to your mind? *Why, God?* Beat yourself up? Start to panic? Look to blame someone? Pray to God for help? Read the story in Exodus 14, and rejoice with the Israelites that God is always working behind the scenes, even if He is not finished with your story yet. Read Exodus 15 about the song of deliverance the Israelites sang.

2. Read and memorize Philippians 1:6; journal your thoughts about it, or share with your group.

3. Do you need God's deliverance from an issue right now? Maybe it is distracting music messages, shopaholic tendencies, workaholic issues, or something else. Begin by saying, "Lord, I give You _____. You have to take it because I don't even have the courage or strength to give it." Claim Exodus 15:13 for yourself: "In your unfailing love you will lead the people you have redeemed. In your strength you will guide them to your holy dwelling."

If you do not recognize any issues, that is all right. It may not be time to view them yet. Pray for God to bless you with the friends He thinks you need, friends who take joy in uplifting you in prayer.

Or maybe you observe an issue in someone else. Recognize that God is working from the inside out, and he or she may not see it yet. Pray right now for the person to recognize the issue and give it over to God. Claim Exodus 15:13 for this person.

CHAPTER THREE

Don't Get Comfortable!

A person's steps are directed by the LORD.
How then can anyone understand their own way?
—*Proverbs 20:24*

My husband and I settled into a routine of working, enjoying time with family and friends, and church activities. Twelve years flew by while I worked in the credit union industry. The college worship talks and praying-with-people-as-a-ministry years were out of my mind. The credit union motto was "People helping people," and it was a pleasure giving talks about the benefits of credit unions. In the quiet of my mind though, God put the thought of something else, something like women's ministries. One day I told God, "I'm comfortable, and I'm staying here at the credit union until the current manager retires. However, if You want to move me into something else, go right ahead." God is not surprised by our statements or challenged to carry out His plan when we give Him our lives.

Paving the way

Have you ever thrown God a challenge or asked God for guidance? He *loves* to interact with us. Sometimes we see it right away; sometimes He works behind the scenes. One of my new friends, Julie, "pressured" me to go to a women's retreat in October 1998. Another friend had tried the previous two years. Both times I retorted, "The women just gossip and cry the whole time, and that's not my thing." Julie gave the same response as the previous person. "Not all women gossip and cry." So out of loyalty to our friendship, I went. At the first meeting, I was smack-dab in the middle of the pavilion with hundreds of women when the Holy Spirit said to me, *"Go to the prayer room!"* It was a loud command from God.

Lord, we can pray anywhere. I don't have to go to the prayer room! I asserted.

God did not give up. At the end of the meeting, Julie looked over at me gleefully. "Diane, let's go to the prayer room." Well, hindsight being twenty-twenty and clueless me not understanding that God was now trying to intervene and speak to me through someone else, I retorted, "But Julie, we can go anywhere to pray." I proceeded to list some nice places, such as benches outside on the bike path and the home where we were staying. Adding with some finality, I said, "So, you see, we don't need to go to the prayer room!" Her face saddened, and I thought she might cry.

The next day *God through her* tried again when Julie said, "Diane, let's go to the anointing service to see what it's like." Well, if I was not going to go to the prayer room, I surely was not going to attend an anointing service. I do not remember my reply, but I do remember her hurt look. Conversely, I was really enjoying the retreat speaker who spoke about prayer. Before one of the meetings, a woman I had never seen before, Corleen Johnson (the director of Women's Ministries for the Oregon Conference), got up to speak. I made a comment about her to God in my mind. The Holy Spirit was quick to reply, *"You will be working with her next year."* It seemed odd, since I had a job I liked. I could not think of a snappy comeback for that one.

In the car, on the way home from that retreat, my friends Julie and Jan, who were prayer partners, were talking. They had apparently been praying behind the scenes for me because, unexpectedly, I blurted out, "I think I'm ready for a prayer partner in my life. Can we pray that God will find me one?"

Take note. If you pray that prayer, your life will never, ever (did I stress that enough?) be the same! Little did I realize it at the time, but God was working to intervene dramatically in my life.

"Do you have someone in mind for a prayer partner, Diane?" Jan asked.

"Yes; actually I do." I told her a name. "However, I want God to choose because He knows best," I replied. Several days later I called the woman and asked if we could meet. "I think God has brought me to the place where I would like to pray with someone on a regular basis, like a prayer partner. Would you be my prayer partner?" I asked.

"Yes, I can sense that this is what God is telling me to do," she responded.

Practical prayer tips

I was not sure how this new way of praying differed from praying alone. As I set out in earnest, looking for a book or something, I found a little book on prayer partnering called *Two Are Better Than One,* by David Mains and Steve Bell.

I liked these reasons for having a prayer partner:

- New ministries and opportunities will unfold for you.
- Every Christian has a weak side; but if you have a prayer partner, your weakness will probably be your prayer partner's strength. "The Bible speaks about one chasing a thousand, and two putting ten thousand to flight. When you have a prayer partner, you become ten times stronger."[1]
- Point out God's hand in a situation where you may not see it.
- "Rarely will both of you (or the three of you) be struggling in the same areas at the same time. . . . Fresh perspective that provides hope and encouragement is contagious! Everyone benefits when you begin praying with one or two others."[2]

It worked! However, it only worked for six weeks. I noticed that my prayer partner started struggling with personal issues. The devil seeks to discourage us and cause us to doubt that God can change anything in our lives. This becomes very apparent when you attempt a bigger prayer plan. It was a big struggle, and she would leave the room crying at times. The devil knew she would be successful if this continued. "The earnest prayer of a righteous person has great power and produces wonderful results" (James 5:16, NLT). She chose to not continue. It seemed odd to me that God would give me a prayer partner for only six weeks. I really questioned that one and wondered why it hurt so much. I told God, "I'm not going to ask anyone else to be my prayer partner. This failed. If You still want me to have one, You will choose them, and they will ask me!"

Two months later, at a local church's women's retreat, I heard the main speaker say, "Before this retreat, I have been praying for each one of you. And I specifically looked up a verse for you that I believe God chose." She handed us each an envelope. I read my verse, and my heart sank. I knew right then that something awful was going to happen. My verse was,

> "When they call on me, I will answer;
>   I will be with them in trouble.
>   I will rescue and honor them.
> I will reward them with a long life
>   and give them my salvation" (Psalm 91:15, 16, NLT).

Three days later, on February 8, 1999, after spending years in that credit union, God made me want to leave my job and trust Him in the unknown. A situation arose, people pointed fingers, gossip flew, and no one asked the victim for the truth or offered evidence. I chose to stand up for truth and followed the victim right out the door. Later so did several others. It was awful to walk out on a job I enjoyed and that I did not have to give up. However, honesty, justice, and loyalty are more important.

I gave myself to prayer

Like David, I gave myself to prayer. I felt I did not have anything else. It seemed like I had walked into a wilderness alone. Very discouraged, those first few nights I stayed up most of the night reading the Bible and praying.

My second night in the "wilderness," without a job, spent in reading and prayer, was interrupted. An unexpected yellow light bathed the room. An angel suddenly stood by my side, looking at me. "His" head almost reached my nine-foot ceiling. Earthly words are inadequate to describe the care, hope, and compassion that flowed from the eyes and countenance of this angel. Overwhelmingly, I knew God cared that I hurt. He had opened my eyes so I could see how much. Although I did not know my future, He did, and I would soon learn to trust more deeply.

Two months later Lois, one of my college roommates, called and said, "I just moved to town and would like to see you again." God has a sense of humor. It had been thirteen years since I graduated from college. Fourteen since I bid goodbye to Lois Barger when she went to Finland to be a student missionary. She had married a few years earlier, and I was unable to attend. Now she was Lois Meythaler.

The second time I went to visit with Lois, I heard her say, "Would you be my prayer partner?" God apparently still wanted me to have one, and His timing is always perfect.

Where two or three are gathered

Obviously, I had several prayer requests. I needed a job; but more than that, I wanted something that was rewarding. Having a prayer partner quickly became refreshing as I listened to someone else's earnest prayers over what was bothering me. We prayed in person, usually once a week or by phone if urgent things came up. We started a little journal of prayer requests and praises. Now, looking back, I am awestruck at all that happened.

Weeks went by. I remember opening a checking account with a form that had a spot asking for my occupation. It hit me like a ton of bricks. Just what was my identity? Was it my husband's employment? No. And it does not help when your husband asks, "Just what are you going to do with the rest of your life?" I only knew two things:

1. How I spent my days.
2. I had a nagging feeling that I should be in women's ministries.

Sometimes I prayer walked the road by my house. It is a nice country, one-and-a-half-mile road. The first half of it I gave God my list of requests. Many times I would just not say anything after that. I had run out of things to say. Often negative thoughts would crowd in. In order to make them go away, I would go over the same list, this time praising the Lord for something about each one. Essentially, I was "bringing every thought into captivity to the obedience of Christ" (2 Corinthians 10:5, NKJV). Pretty soon I was not plagued by negative thoughts at the end of my road. This created a good habit of praise, and I found I enjoyed praising God for things.

My journal entry for July 5, 1999, says, "Dear heavenly Father, I awoke this morning with such a peace that has remained all day. . . . At 9:05 P.M., Lois phoned and told me she felt the need to pray extra for me that day. It worked."

Why not?

July 7 entry: "I am moving out in faith that God wants me involved in women's ministries." *Doesn't Ione volunteer in women's ministries?* I thought. I looked up her number and picked up the phone. "Ione, this is Diane, do you remember me? . . . Are you connected with women's ministries? I would like to be involved." She definitely remembered me. "Diane, I'm so glad you called. I think you should attend the women's ministries leadership workshop Thursday and Friday at camp meeting in just over a week. Come, and at the end of the meeting, I'll introduce you to Corleen, the director of women's ministries," Ione urged. This seemed to be God's timing. What if I had called two weeks later?

Every step along the way, Lois and I lifted up my direction to God. I wanted to be involved in women's ministries and kept wondering where God was leading my life. "Will you pray for me on Thursday?" I called three people for prayer before I walked into the leadership workshop. Upon entering, I noticed a display that women's ministries had set up about the Philippines. Drawn to the display, I walked over and grabbed a brochure. It was an invitation to be a part of an evangelistic team of people traveling to Kidapawan City, Philippines, in March 2000. When I realized what I was looking at, I wanted to get the first word in with God. Oblivious to others around me, I raised my fist with the brochure in my hand, "No! Don't make me go!" Next, my practical nature sat down with the brochure and said, "Well if I did go, what would I do?" Scanning the needs list, I saw volunteers were wanted for a health clinic, children's ministries, family life talks, and Bible studies. I wasn't any of those people. Someone else could do all those things better. "Lord, I don't know how to do Bible studies, but maybe I could learn."

Some meetings can change your life

The leadership meeting began, and I was inspired by many of the speakers. Afterward Ione introduced me to Corleen. "Would you like to be on our women's retreat committee?" Corleen asked. A little surprised by my sudden good fortune, or now what I would call a "God moment," I did not respond with a yes or a no.

"What do they do?" I asked.

"Oh, we get together once a month to plan the annual Christian women's retreat. It is not far away," she responded.

"OK, I can be on your committee." That night I called my friend Julie to express happy sarcasm. "Now I have a once-a-month volunteer job called the women's retreat committee."

"Oh, Diane, have faith. Just wait; you are soon going to be busier than ever," she replied. Little did she know that she was a prophetess.

The teeny, tiny window of opportunity called the women's retreat committee would become a large picture window with a view of what God can accomplish if I am willing.

Moments of Reflection:

1. Did the Holy Spirit bring to mind anyone that God has used to speak to you? Did you resist that person? Or ask God if what he or she said was a valid statement and lift it up in prayer?

2. Maybe right now you are challenging God to do something new in your life. Take pen and paper, or your computer, and jot down a few ways God has led in the past. Then, while "bringing every thought into captivity"

(2 Corinthians 10:5, NKJV), write down what you think might be happening now, and praise Him in advance for what He will do.

3. Do you know anyone you might like to ask to be your prayer partner once a week or so? Pray about it. If you still feel compelled, ask that person.

---

1. David Mains and Steve Bell, *Two Are Better Than One* (Colorado Springs, CO: Multnomah, 1991), 8.
2. Ibid., 12.

CHAPTER FOUR

Changing Direction Takes a Few Adjustments!

*Whether you turn to the right or to the left, your ears will hear
a voice behind you, saying, "This is the way; walk in it."*
—*Isaiah 30:21*

Knowing God wanted me involved in women's ministries, I thought, *Wouldn't it be helpful to have a master's in this?* So I applied at a biblical seminary on August 13, 1999. To my great surprise, two weeks later the academic dean asked to meet with me to go over my application. Holding my application in his hand, as I nervously sat on the other side of his desk on August 30, he read my personal statement. "When we step out of our comfort zone and seek out something we have been curious about, sometimes it changes our whole life's direction. I would never want to limit God as to my future direction in life. I believe as we grow and change He opens new avenues for us. I learn new tools and concepts as God continues to help people through me." We engaged in discussion about my future and why I wanted to be at the seminary and imagine my surprise when he replied, "I don't think this is what you need to do."

Slam went that door. Still stunned by this, several hours later I went to my first women's retreat committee meeting at the conference office. As Corleen introduced me, she asked me to share a little about myself. I included what happened earlier that day. "Diane, we can train you in women's ministries right here," was her response. Apparently, God thought so too.

Laying the groundwork

As I listened to their retreat plans, someone said, "Diane could be on the prayer team." I heard myself respond, "Yes, and maybe my friend Lois can help too." How ironic this was. Last year I emphatically told Julie, "No, I won't go to the prayer room." Not only that, as they explained the anointing service, I felt compelled to be anointed for my sinuses. There were two things I was quickly learning.

1. It is better to just pray and get out of God's way.
2. When we tell God what we will not do, we frequently end up doing that very thing and liking it.

God surely laughed at me; however, He was not done with surprises. Three days later, on Thursday, September 2, 1999, I was amazed by His words in my head, *"Go to the conference office at 10:00 A.M. on Tuesday." What does that mean?* I wondered. "You'll never guess what God wants me to do now," I shared with one friend as I asked her to join me in prayer for that day. Two other friends also promised to pray. The Holy Spirit did not say what to do when I got to the Oregon Conference office at 10:00 A.M., *"Just go, and trust Me!"* What a test of faith!

"Hello, Raneé," I said to the receptionist as I entered the building and walked up to her desk.

"Diane, I just know the Lord has sent you to us today." This statement caught me off guard. I knew God sent me. Why would she say it? I did not have long to wonder. She knew I was currently out of work. "Diane, what are you doing with yourself now?"

"Well, I volunteer at the community center on Thursdays, and that's about it," I replied.

"So you're free on Wednesdays? We need a receptionist for that day. Would you be interested?" she asked.

God, is this a test? I don't really want to do this, I prayed in my mind. No response came. I mused, *Sure, where is God with His quick responses now?* I needed to say something, "Sure, I could probably do that."

Raneé immediately picked up the phone and called Nancy, the Human Resources director, who was not in. "That's OK. Would you direct me to Women's Ministries? I'll come back and check with you later," I promised.

"Hi, Wanda, I'm here to help you," I expressed confidently as I approached the Women's Ministries Department. Wanda Krein, the Women's Ministries assistant, was not expecting me. Simultaneously, as Wanda shared that she could really use my help, Corleen quickly strode out of her office to greet me. This was only my third time to meet her. Now she startled me by putting her arms around me in a hug.

"You're going to help us? We could sure use it. We're behind on a few things getting ready for the retreat."

Wanda gave me a desk next to hers and a pile of envelopes with retreat applications and checks. My head began to pound. A sinus headache throbbed within, and I was sniffing like I had to blow my nose; doing God's work does not automatically remove our pain. A very long forty-five minutes later, I remembered Raneé and wondered what she had found out. "I'm going to go to the restroom and get some tissues," I told Wanda while thinking, *I can check with Raneé at the same time.*

"Here are some tissues right here," Wanda replied.

Oh no, I thought. Fifteen minutes later I mustered my courage to say, "Actually, I need to talk to Raneé. Would you get her on the phone for me?"

"Raneé, it looks like I will be helping here for a while. Would you page me when Nancy wants to meet with me?" What seemed like hours since my head was pounding was probably only minutes.

"I'm going to go to lunch now. What are you going to do?" asked Wanda. Thinking that was a good idea, I also went. Raneé found me in the hall and rushed me to Nancy's office. However, on the way there, she threw in a curve.

She whispered, "Wanda also wants the reception job."

Then why was she so anxious to have me interview? I wondered.

"So you want to be a receptionist?" Nancy asked. I did not really want to be, but I heard myself saying, "I am interested, but I would not want to take the job if Wanda wants it."

She quickly came back with, "We also have a position open for an assistant in the Education Department. Would you be interested in that?" I knew I did not want to do that either. Even though I was out of work, I did not feel the Education Department was my calling.

"You know, I really think my passion is women's ministries and that is what God is leading me toward, so I would have to say no to the education position," I responded.

"This morning Wanda came to my office. She wants to retire in April. She wanted the receptionist job so she could have it after she retired from Women's Ministries. Would you be interested in her job in April?" Nancy asked.

"Oh, yes, definitely, that would be great," I responded. Indeed, this was a surprise, and now I had a small glimpse of God's plan. *But, Lord, what am I going to do between now and April?* I prayed my petition silently.

Back at Women's Ministries after lunch, I grabbed some envelopes that needed correct addresses. I headed toward the workroom. Minutes later, Wanda rushed in and pulled up a chair across from me. "Raneé told me you applied for the receptionist position. And Nancy said you were interested in my job. If you are truly interested in my job, I'm going to go to Corleen right now and tell her. You see, I was going to wait until after the October retreat to tell her I was retiring, so she wouldn't have to worry during the retreat."

A bit taken aback that news traveled so fast, I stammered, "Yes, actually, I would like to have your job." Wanda fled from the workroom before I had a chance to change my mind. Imagine Corleen's surprise when Wanda ran in and said, "I'm retiring in April, and I have already found my replacement." I was very intrigued by what Corleen's reaction would be to this news.

"It's been quite a day, hasn't it, Diane?" Corleen asked when I finally ventured back down the hall to Women's Ministries.

"Well, the Lord sent me here today, and three of my friends were praying behind the scenes," I replied.

A month later Nancy phoned me, "I'm calling to let you know we gave the receptionist job to someone else. That is probably disappointing to you."

"No," I replied, "I just figure God has something else for me to do in the meantime." Little did I know it involved three weeks as a missionary in a foreign country.

Moments of Reflection:

1. Need a new direction? Mention it to God in your personal prayers and devotions, and consider praying about it with others. Are you part of a Bible study and prayer group for sharpening your ministry effectiveness?

CHAPTER FIVE

Pleading for Blessings

"Lord, listen! Lord, forgive! Lord, hear and act!
For your sake, my God, do not delay."

—*Daniel 9:19*

O*h, God, You have to pray through me. I don't know what to say. They*
have prayed for everything already, I silently pleaded. Still feeling like
a beginner at prayer, those were my words to God on October 18,
1999. We were having one final committee meeting before the retreat.

"Let's get into a circle and have a prayer for the retreat," Corleen said
excitedly. "Just say a sentence or two about different aspects of the event."
We held hands, and they went around the circle. I dreaded my turn, wondering what I should say. *Uh-oh, it's my turn.* When I opened my mouth,
unexpectedly, words came to me. "Lord, I would ask that You bless the
Sunriver staff, those working behind the scenes. Like the kitchen people and
the clean-up people. May they see You in us and realize they need You in a
deeper way, amen."

The Friday of the retreat, I specifically prayed to God, "I need more help
than usual. These other committee members have helped with this before.
In order to be effective, I need to be in the right place at the right time. And,
Lord, I want to be available to help Corleen when she needs me."

Lois and I arrived in Sunriver at noon. Lois came because I had talked her
into helping me with the prayer walk. We walked into the pavilion where
the retreat committee was setting up for the meeting. Immediately, Corleen
found a need for me to be a gofer between the Great Hall where registration
was taking place and the Pavilion. Arriving back at the Pavilion after several
trips, I found Corleen and several of the committee members discussing an
issue. My problem-solving personality kicked in, and I offered a solution.
Several hours later, after dashing to a nearby city and back to solve the issue,

then attending to more things, I decided I wanted to sit for a moment. Knowing there were nice chairs in the prayer room, I headed that way.

Closing my eyes in the prayer room, I relaxed and started to chat with God. "Oh, I'm sorry, I didn't know you were in here," said one of the Sunriver staff. I opened my eyes to see her walking into the middle of the room.

"Oh, no, feel free; come in, come in," I urged.

"Well, I was just going to straighten some chairs," she replied.

"We have them set pretty much how we want them," I acknowledged. "There are little groupings of two here and three there. This is our prayer room."

She looked around at the pictures of Jesus and pretty things we had placed strategically. "You know, I have always thought this would make a wonderful prayer room," she affirmed.

"What type of work do you do here at Sunriver?" I asked. One thing led to another, and she started sharing her life story. She felt led there from another job. One of her daughters went to church with her, and she felt guilty that the other one had strayed from God. After listening to some more stories, I felt guilty that I was probably keeping her from working. "Well, feel free to come in any time you want to," I urged. "Let me walk you to your next destination so we can keep talking," I suggested. Moments later we reached the cafeteria line. She went one way, and I took up a position in line. "I hope to see you again later," I emphasized to her as she departed. Thinking to myself, *It will never happen.*

Hours later I joined some friends in the main meeting hall just before the program. They wanted to sit on the opposite side of the building and farthest from the door. I felt funny about that but followed them anyway. It had been a long day running around, and it felt good to sit. The speaker was mesmerizing. Her stories drew me in, and I began to relax in my seat. However, God is always on the alert behind the scenes.

Another test, Lord?

"Get out of the building!" I heard. Friends sitting on both sides of me told me later, "You suddenly put your hands to your head and then shot forward out of your seat. We thought you remembered something you didn't do." I remember thinking I felt funny—like I was not supposed to be there. *Still, small Voice—nothing!* The Holy Spirit's voice was loud that time, and it startled me. Everyone else was riveted to their chairs like they had not heard. God wanted to send me on an errand apparently, and I hurried for the door.

There was a beautiful, starry sky. There are more stars visible in Sunriver because it is away from the city. Staring up like I could see God or guess what I was supposed to do next, I asked, "Now what?" I was not expecting a response. *Surely God does not want me to stand out in the cold.* I pondered thoughts in my head. *It's amusing how He sends us out on mini-faith adventures sometimes. The year before I had been so stubborn and refused to go to the prayer room. This must be what God wants now. I need to go there.* Several doors to the building were locked. *I am getting in this building!* Heading to another door, I spotted a little white cord coming out of it. Workers must have put it there. Opening the door, I was startled to find the room dark with no one around. *Surely I am supposed to go in here.* I crept slowly down the hall toward the prayer room, not sure what I would find. Reaching the room, I turned on two lights and thought, *That's odd, no one is here. Why am I here?*

Spotting the chair I sat in earlier, I walked across the room to it. "God, I don't know what I'm supposed to be praying about." I started to ramble about several different things. Then thoughts started to form. *Lord, thank You for giving me a purpose in this retreat. Bless Kay as she is speaking to the women right now and . . . this is rather nice being with You, Lord. Wait! What's that? It sounds like someone is vacuuming down the hall. Lord, that's irritating. Here I am having this nice conversation with You, and now, I'm, I'm—that's why I'm here, isn't it?* I leaped from my chair, headed straight for the vacuum noise where I spotted her around the corner in a room. "Hi, Becky, how are you doing?" The memory came back to me. Earlier when she was sharing with me in the prayer room, she said she was getting off about this time. "Would you like to pray with me in the prayer room?" I asked.

"Yes, I would really like that," she replied. After putting away the vacuum, we headed down the hall. In the prayer room, she spotted the little lamb cards we had on a table. "Please take one of those scripture promise cards," I urged.

"All day long I've had this strange feeling that I'm supposed to call my cousin that I haven't talked to in two years. We have drifted apart," Becky said.

"Then this is something we need to pray about," I encouraged.

"I'm nervous to pray with others. Could you just pray?" she asked.

"Of course," I answered. I prayed for her relationship with her cousin and some things I remembered from our earlier conversation. It is amazing how quickly God puts us to work when we show the tiniest hint that we are willing. "OK, now maybe you should go and call your cousin. I will be eager to hear what happens," I suggested as we left the prayer room.

The next morning began early. Slipping to my knees, I sought direction from God. "Lord, You did so much for me yesterday. Please do the same again today. I need to be in the right place at the right time again. That really worked yesterday. Please bless Corleen, and help me effectively assist her."

Lois and I went to the prayer room to meet the prayer team and pray over requests. Many had been turned in with various needs. During our prayer session, I prayed. "Lord, place Becky in my path today if You want me to hear the ending of the story." Walking out of the room, I saw Becky about forty feet away. "Becky, what happened?" I asked.

"You would not believe it," Becky joyously explained, "Had I gone straight home, I would have missed my cousin and been too tired to place the call again. But because we took time to pray, God must have done a miracle because my cousin had just walked in the door, and we chatted for over an hour. God gave us healing in our relationship. We are going to be e-mailing one another from now on. I was so excited I couldn't sleep."

Praise the Lord for His goodness. Becky never told me what caused the estrangement with her cousin. All that mattered was that God had performed a miracle of healing in their relationship.

I believe

Mark 9:24 says, "Lord, I believe; help my unbelief!" (NKJV). This was the kind of belief I needed as I headed to the anointing service with Lois and another friend. Imagine how interesting it looked from heaven's vantage point. "Hey, look, the one that refused to go to the anointing service last year with Julie, is going now. Let's see what God is going to do." They all pressed in to behold the scene of someone stepping out in faith.

My sinuses had been giving me problems for as long as I could remember. The leaders gave women the opportunity to share before they formed little prayer groups. Many were tearful as they recalled past anointing services. Some had been healed. Others reflected they felt peace and spiritual healing but not physical healing. It was nice, but honestly it was too long, for two reasons. I was a little tense and nervous about the unknown, and my mind wandered and started counting exactly how many minutes I had before the next event—the prayer walk Lois and I were leading. This was another first for me, so I was not sure how it would turn out.

"Let's have a word of prayer before we break into our groups," Corleen said. I focused again on the situation; I had asked Ione Richardson to anoint me.

"Diane, how about if you pray first and share with God your request before the others in our circle pray," she said.

"Lord, I want to be in service for You, and this sinus thing hinders me. I'll live with it, if You want. However, if I could do more effective service, please heal me," I pleaded. Everyone in my little group said a beautiful prayer before Ione ended and then applied oil on my forehead. They followed exactly what it said to do in James 5:14, "Is anyone among you sick? Let him call for the elders of the church, and let them pray over him, anointing him with oil in the name of the Lord" (NKJV).

Many have wondered what happens when people are anointed. Some have said, "I felt a warming." Some have said, "I knew I was instantly healed." Others were not healed physically, but over time they noticed spiritual changes. I didn't have time to wonder what, if anything, had happened. Lois and I left quickly to lead the prayer walk, and God blessed our efforts.

During the prayer walk, I kept noticing something smelled very smoky to me even though there was no smoke in the air that day. It was not until I entered a building later that the smell overwhelmed me. I started coughing and then realized, *The smoke smell is coming out of my nose.* Sounds strange and, in retrospect, I should have run to a mirror. My God *had* done something to my sinuses, and time would show that I would never have a sinus headache again.

The missing coat

My prayer to be in the right place at the right time was really paying off. Here it was Sunday already, and we were packing up to leave. Hauling out some items from the Great Hall, I ran into Corleen heading my direction out of the Pavilion. Spotting me outside, she shared, "I lost my coat yesterday, and many people have tried to find it. We have combed every room in the Great Hall, but with no results. You know what it looks like, don't you? It's white and long and has pockets. Would you see if you can find it?"

Oh my! This is a tall order. I'm not even attempting this by myself. These were my thoughts as I walked back toward the Great Hall. "Lord, You know exactly where her coat is. You can see it as we speak. Corleen needs it. Show me where it is!" Just as soon as I said this, a flash happened in my brain. A mental picture came into my mind, and I saw the coat hanging over a chair in the mechanical room. Just as quickly, I brushed aside the picture, thinking, *That's not logical.* Why would it be in there? So I took a cursory glance through the Great Hall and went toward the lodge. The Sunriver staff had not seen it. As I walked back toward the Great Hall, I remembered that God gave me a mental picture that I brushed aside. I lamented to God, *I do believe; help me overcome my unbelief!* Excited now, I rushed toward the mechanical room. Of course, it was there, hanging over the chair. Just like the mental picture God gave me. Excitedly, I carried it over my shoulder, walked back outside, and handed it to Corleen.

"Where was it?" she asked with a look of shock.

"Our God knew where it was," I replied, smiling. To which she replied, "What are you doing tomorrow? We have a Monday morning prayer group that meets at my office. Would you like to join us?" Corleen asked me this as I handed her stuff to pack in a vehicle.

"Sure, I could probably be there. That would be nice. Thanks," I responded.

If I thought that things were beginning to be fun and interesting, although at times a little strange, I had not seen anything yet. Get me to pray regularly with a prayer group in addition to my prayer partner and look out—God was only beginning.

Moments of Reflection:

1. James 5:13–17 tells us to "call the elders of the church to pray," when we are sick. Share a story about when you have done this or ponder if you need to have special prayer for a health need.

2. Do you pray to be in the right place at the right time? And then do you move forward in faith that you will be?

CHAPTER SIX

The "Battle" Behind the Scenes

Put on the full armor of God, so that you can take your stand against the
devil's schemes. For our struggle is not against flesh and blood, but against
the rulers, against the authorities, against the powers of this dark world
and against the spiritual forces of evil in the heavenly realms.
—Ephesians 6:11, 12

Demons were peering at me through a large picture window as I walked up to the Women's Ministries Department for my first prayer group. Annoyed and startled, I looked away and wondered what it meant. It was nerve-wracking, joining a prayer group with experienced prayer women. Two of them had prayed with Women's Ministries almost every Monday morning for fourteen years. They were much older than me and used big words and appropriate scriptures in their prayers. They prayed around the circle; when it came to my turn, it felt like my mouth went dry and my voice sounded awful for much of my turn. In my mind, I prayed, *Lord, I sound so amateur; please help me.* There was no reply; no help seemed to come. There was a strange feeling in the room—a tightness, a darkness—like there was no extra space in the room. I thought it was just the way I felt.

"I'm so glad you came. Please come again next Monday," Corleen urged.

Who is she kidding? I wondered. *They don't need my prayers. They are doing just fine without me. Why is she so eager to have me come?*

All week I had a battle in my head. *Go. Don't go. Go. Don't go.* It was awful! By Monday, God won out, and I went to the prayer group again thinking, *Surely it will get better the second time.* Was I ever wrong! The room still felt strange, dark, and tight. Before they prayed, they spent some time talking and writing down all the prayer needs. Many of the names of the people requesting prayer were unknown to me. How could I pray for people I did not know? Waiting through this list prolonged my agony. *Lord, please help me. I really need Your help,* I prayed in my head in the interim. Beth Coffin, our prayer group leader, shared a devotional thought before we began praying.

Glancing at Corleen, I wondered, *Why does she keep looking at her watch? Is she in a hurry?* But what did I know? They were the experts, so I did not say anything about their protocol.

Oh no! What's happening? Lord, I feel tense enough, and now I am hearing one of them in a foreign language, I pleaded with God. *What is the reason for this?* This time as we went around the circle, when one of them prayed, her words came out in a foreign language. I opened my eyes. No one else seemed to hear this or be disturbed by anything. So I did not tell anyone about this experience, and I left with Corleen's words in my head. *"I'm so glad you came. I hope you can come next Monday."*

Who am I supposed to talk to about hearing someone in tongues while they prayed? I thought.

Besides the Monday Women's Ministries group, Lois and I also met for prayer once a week. Twice I shared with Lois that the Women's Ministries Department had mentioned a mission trip to the Philippines. "Every time they mention the Philippines, I feel a strange nudging. We need to pray for the Holy Spirit to make it obvious if I'm supposed to go."

By the third time I went to the Monday morning prayer group, I was feeling somewhat "battle" weary. Ephesians 6:12 says, "For our struggle is not against flesh and blood, but against the rulers, against the authorities, against the powers of this dark world and against the spiritual forces of evil in the heavenly realms." It was "the spiritual forces of evil in the heavenly realms" that were oppressing me. They did not want me to join this new prayer group. Ron Halvorsen, in his book *Prayer Warriors,* has a section in chapter 7 where he describes earth.

Battleground earth is a no-man's land where great, unseen forces are still locked in battle. The work of Prayer Warriors is but the human side of the battle. God's word pulls back the curtain and lets us glimpse the reality of other forces at work:

And after these things I saw four angels standing on the four corners of the earth, holding the four winds of the earth, that the wind should not blow on the earth, nor on the sea, nor on any tree. And I saw another angel ascending from the east, having the seal of the living God, and he cried out with a loud voice to the four angels to whom it was given to hurt the earth and the sea, saying, Hurt not the earth, neither the sea, nor the trees, till we have sealed the servants of our God in their foreheads.—Revelation 7:1-3 [KJV].

Look closely at what this is saying: The destructive powers are being held back in order that God's Prayer Warriors may have the work of redemption fully accomplished in their lives and in the lives of others: You and I have a striking role in this process. . . . By opening our lives to God's Spirit and His work, by diligent intercession for others, we can give God's angel armies access to humanity and to life situations so that they can do their work.[1]

Despite the fact that I knew all heaven was with me and I was a prayer warrior intercessor in my group, I still felt all alone, with no one to tell about the behind-the-scenes battle. That third Monday, as I approached the Women's Ministries Department, I looked out the windows and through the Holy Spirit's power I could see the powers of darkness again. There was a huge picture window that looked out on to the grounds, and I could see actual demons peering back at me, thus the battle feeling. They had been there the other times. In fact, they had also peered in the prayer room window.

This time when we prayed around the circle, the same person spoke in tongues again. *Lord, look, I'm tense enough just being here with these experienced pray-ers, and this makes me feel worse because I don't understand it. Why am I hearing her in a foreign language? Please turn it off!* I demanded to God in my head. He took mercy on me. Every time after that I heard her in my language, English. However, the room still had a strange, crowded, dark feeling that I could not shake. There was no one to talk with about this.

One night I attended a Bible study with eight or ten women from my church. The study group was deep into the discussion when I heard the Holy Spirit, *"When are you going to learn to give Bible studies?"*

Excuse me, but I'm in a Bible study, I replied in my head. No use, He had grabbed my attention, so I continued, *Lord, the only person I know that could teach me is Ione Richardson, and I don't know her number off the top of my head.* Of course, He reminded me of the number; God knows everyone's number. I grabbed my cell phone and went out the front door.

Looking up at the black night sky, I said, "You want me to go to the Philippines, don't You?" Indeed, teaching Bible studies was the only thing I had reasoned I could do that day in July at the women's ministries leadership workshop. I placed the call.

"Ione, I think I'm supposed to go to the Philippines. Would you teach me to give Bible studies?" I asked. If you know Ione, you know her willing reply. "Yes, I'll teach you what I have learned." Two nights later I was at her house, asking, "Do you think the Monday prayer group is a good time to tell Corleen I'm interested in the Philippines?"

"Yes, and I can't wait till Monday to see her response," Ione agreed.

Opposition arose on my way to the prayer group as a huge truck roared up from behind me on Monday morning. There were two lanes going up a hill, and an unknown driver got beside me and started to crowd me. Then he swerved into me. Thankfully, I glimpsed him coming my way and steered toward the shoulder. *The devil doesn't want me to get to this prayer group,* I thought. My defenses kicked in, *This is more important than I thought. The devil knows I am about to tell the group, "I'm going to the Philippines." He is trying to stop me.*

"My God has already won the victory!" I shouted and claimed it out loud. When I arrived, Ione eagerly looked across the table at me, waiting for me to tell Corleen I was going to the Philippines. I was waiting for the right opportunity. Apparently, so was the battle behind the scenes as many angels, good and bad, were crowded in the room. To me the "battle" feeling was palpable and annoying.

Suddenly, there was a pause in the conversation. "I think God wants me to go to the Philippines," I blurted out. At the split second that I said, "God wants . . . ," it felt like the room had divided in half. It was the oddest feeling. Suddenly, it all became clear to me: demons had fled the room. Only God's angels were left, and peace washed over me. No longer dark and tight, after that, the room was a peaceful place.

I'm doing *what*?

Corleen was so glad I wanted to go that she handed me an application right after the prayer group. Never having gone on a mission trip before, I did not claim to have any qualifications for going. One of the sentences said, "Give a detailed description of how you could serve in the above selected area of ministry." I checked "home visitation" and the word "other" and marked "see below," adding,

Somewhere along the line, I told God to feel free to touch as many people as He wanted through me. I have never met so many people in my life. Now, I hear Him calling me to give Bible studies in the Philippines. I could tell you what else I am good at: problem solving, facilitating, organizing, praying, etc. However, being specific is limiting God. I know He is just trying to get my feet in the door. He keeps assigning me tasks that involve situations/problems I have never encountered before. And I am learning to pray and get out of His way.

"Corleen, is there anything I can help you with?" I asked her the next week as I handed my application back.

"Would you like to come with me to Centralia, Washington, on December 3? Jan White and I are going to do some planning for our Philippines trip."

On Friday, December 3, Corleen dropped by my house to pick me up and then drove to see Jan White. Jan worked as the North Pacific Union Conference Women's Ministries director and would be our evangelistic speaker.

"A mission trip is the perfect thing to awaken the Holy Spirit within," one of my friends told me when I shared I was going. I did not know exactly what she meant, but it sounded mysterious and wonderful. I recalled this as I listened to Jan and Corleen talk about who had applied and what they would be doing for our team. Then they both looked at me. "Would you like to be the coordinator for the trip?"

They must have discussed this together beforehand, I thought. "Oh, I could probably do that," I replied calmly, though I did not feel calm inside.

That night after Corleen dropped me off at my house, I went downstairs to pray in a quiet place. I lay flat on the floor, praying, "You want *me* to coordinate a mission trip? Oh, God, You know I have never been on a mission trip before, let alone coordinated one. I'm not sure what coordinating means, but You know. So You have to do it all. You're the One in charge and these are Your people You are taking to the Philippines. Show me everything step by step. I need to know what to pack, I need to know what to do next . . ." My list went on and on. Standing up and reaching for my Bible, I found,

> Trust in the LORD with all your heart,
> And lean not on your own understanding;
> In all your ways acknowledge Him,
> And He shall direct your paths (Proverbs 3:5, 6, NKJV).

This became my daily mantra. It soothed my soul.

One of the first calls I placed was to Ginny, my travel agent. "We have eight people who need to fly out of Portland and get to Davao, Philippines," I said.

"It can't be done," she replied. "Your return flight falls on spring break weekend, and that flight is booked."

Good, I thought*, now God has a challenge to solve because we need to come back March 26 since most people work the next day.* I prayed about it and decided to focus on something else. A few days later I phoned again and said, "Would you check those dates again to see if we can now fly back on Sunday?"

"I'll send you some itineraries," she responded. She kept giving me itineraries that showed us coming back on Monday. I kept thinking, *Our God can get us back on Sunday.* Finally, I told Corleen, "I'm having trouble getting tickets for the right day." We prayed about it.

On December 29, I suddenly felt compelled that we needed to decide about the tickets. "Ginny, please check again for a way into Portland on March 26," I said to the travel agent.

"There are no flights coming back that day," she replied.

"All right, I'll call you back later," I replied. Now I was desperate and laid on the floor, staring at the ceiling, and pondered. *Lord, I need Your help.* I heard myself say, "I'm not moving from the floor and will remain here praying until You share how You are going to fix this." Forty-five minutes later my phone rang, and it was the travel agent. "I was watching my screen just now and a flight just opened up. You can come back on March 26."

"We'll take it," I replied ecstatically.

Moments of Reflection:

1. Share with your group or journal about a time when you had to trust in the Lord because you did not know how to proceed. Take time to memorize Proverbs 3:5, 6 in a Bible version you like.

2. Is God nudging you to step out in faith right now? What is He nudging you to do? Are you asking the Holy Spirit to guide you by opening or closing "doors"?

---

1. Ron Halvorsen, *Prayer Warriors* (Fallbrook, CA: Hart Research Center, 1995), 76.

CHAPTER SEVEN

Create in Me a Clean Heart

Create in me a clean heart, O God. Renew a loyal spirit within me.
—Psalm 51:10, NLT

Y ou should do something more important than be a volunteer. You can make better use of your time," helpful friends asserted. However, I believed the whole point was to be Christ's servant. Every time I went to the local community center, I pictured Christ ministering to people. What could be better?

The community center started the day with a devotion anyone could attend before people dispersed to their various locations. One hectic morning while planning for the Philippines trip, I called Lois on my way to the community center. "Lois, I have way too many errands for the mission trip to come pray with you today. And I'm probably going to get to the center late."

"You do have a lot to do," she confirmed. "We can pray next week."

As I reached the community center late and entered through the back door, I noticed it was all quiet. *They must still be in worship,* I thought. Continuing in that direction, I entered the room right before the worship room and walked right into an invisible wall, stopping suddenly ten feet before the door. My hands moved up beside me to feel what was happening as my body jerked to a stop. It felt like an invisible wall. Just then my ears heard someone praying. Glancing toward the door, there was a tall angel bending over as if listening to the same prayer I heard. The presence of God washed over me as I realized God was letting me see and feel again what really goes on behind the scenes. The devil was trying to keep me from prayers with this group and Lois.

Astonished that I allowed my to-do list to distract me, and even more amazed that God just showed me what happens behind the scenes, I turned right around and ran to my car for my cell phone. "Lois, I'm coming. I have *felt* the power of prayer," I gushed.

"Oh, I knew you would change your mind and want to pray," she replied.

Prayer is most important

God used the hitting-the-prayer-wall example to instill the idea that prayer is more important than the ever-present to-do list. A few days later, while this was still fresh in my mind, Julie phoned to say, "I'm going to a prayer conference in California called Prayer Works. It's almost a weeklong event in early February. Will you come with me?"

Is she serious? Doesn't she know how much I have to do? When I mentioned the event to Corleen and how close it was to our Philippines trip, she said, "This is something I've decided to attend. You should come too."

"I guess if you think there's time to fit it in, then I should too," I replied.

Thankfully, God keeps working with us no matter what we are doing. He intervenes with different pieces until He makes a beautiful picture. And just when we think we have enough to do, He throws in another puzzle piece. As I prayed about the prayer conference versus staying home and working on the to-do list, I felt peace that I should go to California.

Transformation begins

While at the prayer conference, one of the leaders talked about the text of Psalm 51:10: "Create in me a clean heart, O God. Renew a loyal spirit within me" (NLT). It was also one of the songs we sang at a meeting. This thought worked into my subconscious, and I started repeating it out loud. If you have ever been to a prayer conference, then you can attest that God uses these moments and Scriptures to reveal to us "strongholds" that need to be dealt with in our lives. Even ones you do not know you have; rather like an onion with many layers. It is His purpose to bring healing and transformation to everyone.

Lois called me one day and said, "Diane, I've felt impressed this week to memorize Psalm 51."

"That's strange," I said. "Psalm 51:10 keeps going through my head because one of the leaders here mentioned it, and we have sung it."

"I'm going to fast from chocolate while you are in the Philippines in addition to praying for you," she said a few days later as I was sharing about the prayer conference.

"That's it? Just one food item?" I questioned.

"This will make a difference, Diane," she responded.

Transforming others

After one particular meeting, I felt very uncomfortable and could not place the feeling. I finally drove off in the car and drove ten minutes into what seemed like miles and miles of orange groves. I stopped in the parking lot of an industrial building. Feeling impressed that I was where I was supposed to be, I stayed in the car and just prayed for everything that came to my mind. Fifteen minutes later a car suddenly approached fast from the west and stopped by the curb about fifteen feet from me. Five seconds later another car approached fast from the opposite direction and stopped next to the curb in front of the first car. The two men jumped out, exchanged packages, ran back to their cars, and sped off.

Amazed by this, and thankful they had not seen me, I said, "Lord, I apparently just saw a drug deal go down. You needed someone to pray they will get out of the drug trade. I claim the blood of Jesus Christ over these two men and their families that they will come clean and learn about the difference You can make in their lives." God must have done something, or He would not have sent me. Turning on the engine and driving off, I arrived at the church, walked in, and spotted my small-group Bible study leader. "Peggy, you'll never guess what I just saw take place." Out spilled the story. "Diane, you were responsive to God's Spirit. That is an amazing story! Say, we are having a prayer service and prayer walk around the streets of my church in a few days. Will you come and be my prayer partner for this?" Peggy replied. Stunned that my story had turned into a unique opportunity, I said, "Sure, I would like that."

Create in me a clean heart

The very last day of our prayer conference, as I was listening to the morning meeting, I started feeling uncomfortable again. At the end of the meeting, instead of going to a nice potluck with everyone, I got in the car again. This time I left for the home where I was staying. No one was around, and I made a peanut butter and jelly sandwich and went out the door for a walk to pray about my uncomfortable feeling. About an hour later, I was back at the house still feeling uncomfortable and went to my room and knelt by the bed. "Lord, 'create in me a clean heart, O God. Renew a loyal spirit within me.' That is our emphasis this week, and something is making me uncomfortable. I need Your help."

Suddenly, a memory, apparently long forgotten, flashed into my mind of a time when someone tried to kill me as a child by holding me under water. I had struggled and broken free, and hate filled my heart; but I had not thought about it since. Words I must have never said spilled from my mouth, "Lord, I forgive them, I forgive them," over and over as peace washed over me. It was a forgotten thing, but God knew the bitterness of long ago was still inside me. It is amazing that something from long ago can still cloud our hearts even when we have long forgotten it. Jesus wants every part of our lives, so we can live in peace.

One is good; however, two are better

Three days later, after the prayer conference, while interviewing a client at the community center, a demon suddenly appeared from within the client and peered at me through his eyes. Since I had seen this in other clients, I began to notice it often happened to those possessed by demons when I asked what their spiritual resources were. If they responded, "I attend a group that uses a higher power," instead of naming Jesus, then demons would peer out of their eyes at me. As if to say, "I am the higher power." The experience made me feel like I was in a time-warp tunnel. You can look away, but the ominous feeling does not go away. *My God is stronger,* I thought and looked back. *I need not be afraid. Lord, You need to make this demon go away!* Praying silently seemed to do nothing. I did not want to alarm the people because I knew they could not tell a demon peered out of their eyes, and I was not sure I wanted to tell them, so I ushered the clients out quickly. This experience made me angry, and I began to think, *If things such as this can happen here in my own country, surely even stranger things will happen to me in a foreign country. Since Lois can't go with me, I really need a prayer partner in the Philippines.*

On Monday morning, at my prayer group, I related this story to the ladies, then asked, "Corleen, will you be my prayer partner?"

"I'd be happy to be your prayer partner," she replied. I never would have asked her if this new, scary event had not happened again. God was directing for a lifetime of many incredible answers to prayer because of this new prayer partnership.

Moments of Reflection:

1. Turn to Ephesians 6:10–20, and read it again as a promise for yourself. Journal any thoughts or share with your group any ideas that come to mind. Where do you see any battlefields in your life? In friends' lives? Your community? Your country? Pray, pray, pray.

2. Is there anything God is calling you to do that you are hesitating about? Write down or share with a friend or group how you intend to follow through and uphold your conviction to the Lord. "Lord, I intend to

_____."

3. Read Psalm 51:10–12 as a prayer. Is there is anything you are holding on to that God wants to reveal in your life? Give God time if He does not point out something right away.

CHAPTER EIGHT

Praying to Be a Blessing

Whatever your hand finds to do, do it with all your might.
—Ecclesiastes 9:10

Women need to have the opportunity of personally sharing their love for Christ in their own words, in their own way; to have the opportunity to experience a mission trip where they are the ones presenting the gospel of Jesus Christ," Corleen asserted at our first layover, in Los Angeles. We had gathered for a prayer time to ask for God's Spirit to be poured out on us. It was March 5, 2000, when the first women's evangelistic team from the North Pacific Union Conference left for Kidapawan City, Philippines. Our team included nine women, three men, and a ten-year-old boy.

Heights and incredible views just thrill my soul, and I am usually fine with some turbulence (emphasis on *some*); but somewhere between Hawaii and Manila, over the Pacific Ocean, our plane literally shook like a leaf for a very long time. Many Filipinos on the plane clutched their rosary beads and mouthed words I could not understand. Corleen thought it was humorous that we had to hold on to our food and drink or it would fly away, and she started laughing. *Does she really think this is funny?* I thought. (It was not until months later I figured out that she laughs when she's nervous.) Thankfully, her laughter made me laugh also, easing some of my tension. I thought, *I'm so glad we assigned home-team intercessors to pray for us each step along the way.*

The adventure begins

Jan, her husband Phil, and their kids joined us in Manila, and soon we reached the Davao, Philippines, airport. A beautiful sight awaited us. A crowd was gathered on the street below the window. Many people held on to a huge banner that said, "Welcome, Director for Women's Ministries, Jan White, Christ is the Answer," and the names of all the team members.

This was Jan White's first experience being the speaker for an evangelistic series. "I can't believe we're finally here," she said to Corleen when we arrived four hours later in Kidapawan City. Many had waited hours to greet us with local food and hospitality. Despite our tiredness, the locals were eager to have a meeting with us, so we stopped at a local church on the way to the hotel. The next day we gathered in a circle around Jan and lifted her up in prayer. A couple of weeks later Jan said, "It was a real privilege. I had never preached an evangelistic series before, and it was a stretch for me when Corleen suggested that we do a mission trip. What God did through us was just so amazing. I can't wait until the kingdom of God to see the complete results."

Parade and rally

To advertise our meetings, we involved the whole city in a parade, which also gave us the opportunity to mingle with the people. The children from area schools had created anti-drug-abuse posters that they carried. Bands played, baton twirlers twisted and swayed, and kids as young as five and six years old were dressed smartly in uniforms and marched proudly. We were the ones who stepped out of formation to shake hands and give people leaflets about our event called Jesus Is the Answer. It was a very noisy day with bands, buses, motorcycles, and children all making noise. People in jeepneys (rebuilt World War II jeeps) and tricycles (motorcycles with a sidecar and roof attached) pulled over and eagerly reached out for a brochure.

Me, a judge?

Our parade culminated a huge celebration in a gym, where everyone was seated. Jan presented the mayor of the city with a beautiful picture book of Washington State. On the sidelines, one of our sponsors approached me and three others, saying, "We want you to be judges," then motioned for us to follow. *What is God getting me into now?* The four of us were shown to a table with chairs, and we sat down, not quite sure what we were judging. There were probably about a thousand people in chairs all pointed forward, and we were at a table with the audience on the right and the stage on the left where the activities took place. *We have the best seats in the house,* I thought, astonished. Just then someone approached me and held out a short box, saying, "You take." I peered in at the crackers and orange soda and glanced around the gym. No one else was eating food or drinking soda. After the long parade in the very hot sun, with no water, I took the orange soda and crackers, wondered at my good fortune, and decided I liked being a judge. We still did not know what we were judging. Opening speeches were made, music was played, and then someone motioned to us "judges," and we followed. Pretty soon it was clear. We were to judge little kids' artwork they had made for drug awareness. Suddenly, I did not want to be a judge; it was not fun anymore. I wanted all the kids to win. And if you will excuse a poor parallel, right now I want everyone on earth to win also. The more who hear and accept the good news about Jesus, the more who will not miss out on heaven later.

The meetings

God provided drama one night as Jan was preaching on the fire in Revelation 20. Our teammates, Griffith and Phil, were at the front of the stage, running electronic equipment when smoke appeared to be billowing out from the electronic equipment. They looked over every piece of equipment and everything seemed fine, but smoke continued to billow out. Later we discovered that homeless people under the stage had burnt their supper.

The next day we held a health clinic in the huge gymnasium. As I was standing on the stage where we were setting up the clinic supplies, a darling little girl came up to me and watched everything I did. That evening I grabbed a children's Bible we had brought along and prayed, "Lord, if this is for the little girl, bring her by tomorrow." The next day she was there again, staring at me. "What's your name?" I asked.

"Rochelle," she replied. She did not seem to know any other English words. I wrote her name in the Bible and handed it to her. Her eyes glowed, and her face beamed as she ran from the stage to show some people. She was my best friend after that and showed up for each evening meeting to hold my hand the whole time. I knew she should probably attend the kids' meetings instead of following me on all my background chores, so a couple of nights later I stepped into the children's meeting. Janice Jensen and Sharon Holbrook shared the leadership responsibilities for the children's meetings. A young adult stood watching at the door of the children's meetings each night. He gave his heart to the Lord and was baptized on the last Sabbath.

"The children are so special. I think they have an innocence that we have lost. I guess one of my goals is that we can get back our innocence for Jesus and for each other, which will get us all to the kingdom more quickly," said Janice. "So many children bonded so quickly with us," she stated; and the kids said, "I want to hold your hand when Jesus comes and meet Him together." Forty children responded to the call to walk with Jesus and were baptized.

The few times I sat in on the children's meetings, several mothers attending with their children shocked me by wanting to give me a child. "We heard you and your husband don't have any children. I have talked to my daughter, and she said she would be your daughter. You can take her to America, and she can get a good education there." Deep appreciation for their dedication overwhelmed me. I was humbled at their profound generosity. And still others said, "We are praying for you and your husband. We are so sorry you don't have children."

"It's OK not to have children in America. Many people don't have children," I would respond. They did not understand and still felt so sorry for me, saying, "We will continue to pray that God will help."

The clinic

We quickly fell into a routine with each person "doing" Ecclesiastes 9:10: "Whatever your hand finds to do, do it with all your might."

Before we left home, I was so busy stomping out little "fires" and checking items off our list that I forgot I still did not claim to have any qualifications. However, I knew prayer changes things and "what is impossible with man is possible with God" (Luke 18:27). Now that we were actually in the Philippines, I prayed earnestly, "Lord, please put me in the right place at the right time to be a blessing. In order to do this, I need a double portion of Your Holy Spirit's power." I was in charge of the finances, the prayer group that met before the meetings, and anything else that needed attending. Corleen and I prayed together daily for the needs that arose.

One day the team helped set up the health clinic in the church. Shirley, our team nurse, appeared to have everything under control. All of the donated medicines we had brought along were laid out on a table for dispensing. Drug-resistant tuberculosis is common, and medications are too expensive for most people. About 60 percent of the people treated in the health clinic were infected with some type of roundworm. Many had fungus infections, were diabetic, or had high blood pressure. Several had goiters, asthma, or breast cancer.

Everything looked in order, so Corleen and I left for the hotel. She wanted to practice with Jan and Phil on the song they were to sing that evening. As she was leaving our room to go down to Jan's room, I said, "I feel I need to go back to the clinic. I don't know why, but I just have that feeling."

"Maybe we can go back after lunch. I need to practice," she said. I went to the room and pulled out my expense ledger and receipts to do some figuring. I pulled out my Bible and read; but the feeling remained, so I got down on my knees. "Lord, the feeling won't go away that I am needed at the clinic."

I was certain of it now and headed to Jan's room to share, "Corleen, I'm going to head to the clinic. I'm sure I'll be fine by myself," and turned back toward the door. Our team had been cautioned not to go anywhere alone. There was worry over our safety, so we were hauled everywhere in vans, and we weren't supposed to walk the streets without one of our sponsors with us.

"Wait! I promised myself that I wouldn't let anything happen to you, so I'll go with you," she replied.

Striding down the stairs toward the lobby, I knew I did not know how we were going to get to the church, so imagine my surprise when I saw Tata, the pastor's son, in the lobby.

Assuming God was helping us, I said, "Oh, good, you're here to give us a ride to the church."

"No, he's not," retorted Corleen. "Maybe he is here for something else."

"How long have you been here?" I asked him.

"Forty-five minutes," he responded.

"You see, that was exactly the time I felt the impression to go to the church," I remarked to Corleen.

"Why did you come here?" she asked him.

"Someone said Jan needed a ride," he replied.

"I don't think Jan needs a ride. God sent you for us. Let's go," I said to both of them.

"Wait, let's call Jan to make sure," said Corleen.

I was getting impatient because I knew forty-five minutes had passed and I was needed for something important if God had sent me a ride. Corleen called Jan, and she said, "No, I didn't send for a ride."

At the church, Shirley walked up to me and said, "I have been praying you would come. We are in desperate need of this medication," and she held up a bottle of ampicillin. "No one here has any funds to go get some."

"We'll go get you as much as you need." I took the bottle, glanced around, spotted Viev Leonida, and took off in his direction. Viev was one of the church's elders whom I had met the very first night we arrived. His English was pretty good, although it was still hard to fully understand him. "Viev, would you be able to take Corleen and me on your motorcycle to get some medicine for the clinic? They need it urgently."

We hopped on behind him. As we headed into town on Viev's motorcycle, I felt so exhilarated. I knew I wanted to do this again and prayed we could ride another motorcycle. We had to visit several little pharmacies to get enough of the medicine, and we took their entire supply. It may have cost us fifty dollars, which was about half of a teacher's monthly salary.

Right place, right time

One day, while in our room, I felt impressed to get up and look out the window. *"What do you see?"* the Lord asked me. I thought it was an unusual question because all I could see were five trees. So I remarked, "I see five trees; why?"

"Then that's the time," replied God's voice in my head.

"Time? Time for what?" No response. Sometimes God will answer my first question but not my second question. (Do I ask too many questions?) I turned and looked at Corleen, who I assumed was getting used to my talking out loud with God. I pondered this new information. *I know that the clinic is open at the church today and is supposed to end at five.* Then I spoke my thoughts out loud, "Corleen, I think I'm supposed to go to the church at five." It was about three in the afternoon, and I wondered what would happen. At about 4:30 P.M., black clouds rolled in, and rain poured down. *The devil is trying to dissuade me; this must be important,* I thought. I did not have a ride planned. This was another opportunity to step out in faith. By now I had learned, in a pinch, we could hail a tricycle and get a ride. I began to grab things to go out the door. As I did so, Corleen did too. "You're coming with me?" I asked. "Of course, I wouldn't miss this." Whatever *this* was, we did not know.

I felt compelled to grab one of the Bibles we had brought with us, a nice red one. Dashing out into the rain, one of the hotel workers tried to hail a tricycle for us. The first one almost ran him over. "That was odd; I guess we weren't meant for that one," I mentioned to Corleen. The next one stopped, and the hotel worker told him where we wanted to go. Sitting next to the driver, I made a few casual remarks and then realized he did not speak any English. As I looked around inside his vehicle, I noticed all the idols and suddenly felt very strange. I turned toward Corleen, who had read my mind. She said to me, "I'm already praying for him and his salvation." So I did too.

As we were getting out, I handed him the red Bible and said, even though I knew he could not understand me, "This is a gift for you. Find someone to interpret it for you." Only eternity will reveal what happened with that Bible.

As we stood in the rain, I remarked, "Well, maybe that was why we came. Shall we go back?"

Corleen replied, "No, now that we are here we might as well go in and see what's happening. Maybe we can help do something."

Inside we started talking to different people. Then I noticed Corleen motioning to me. "I want you to meet George," she said. "George is a university student living in a dorm with several others, and he has been sharing the gospel and giving them Bible studies." We prayed with George that God would use him in a big way. I cannot count the times God led us to people with whom He wanted us to pray. What a difference it made to lift their burdens up to God with them. Later we learned that because we encouraged George, he felt inspired to share Jesus with nine of his friends, and they all accepted Jesus and were baptized. Praying to be a blessing resulted in people accepting Jesus into their lives. That's huge!

Moments of Reflection:

1. When the Holy Spirit impresses you to do something for Jesus, don't let the moment pass without responding.

2. How are you sharing Jesus with your friends? With your community?

3. Claim Ecclesiastes 9:10 for yourself, and ask the Lord to give you holy boldness for doing what He puts in front of you.

CHAPTER NINE

Stay on "The Mission"

Be on your guard; stand firm in the faith.
—*1 Corinthians 16:13*

L ions use two hunting styles. In one, the lioness will walk through a herd of zebras and act like she is uninterested in making a kill. Once she finds a weak or vulnerable prey, she ferociously attacks. She roars after the kill. The second hunting style occurs at night. The lion pride waits while a male lion gets on the other side of a herd in plain sight and roars. The panicked herd runs right into the waiting lions. Similarly, Satan attacks from within by using suggestion, and he attacks from the outside by using oppression. In retrospect, although everything was going well, the mission team should have known that danger was lurking.

Each evening I led a little prayer group that met before the meetings. We told our sponsors we would make this gathering available to anyone who wished to meet back stage and pray. A very faithful group of eight to ten Filipino ladies came each night.

Every time we met, I brought something different to share with my little group. I always shared a little devotional thought from the Bible or a devotional book that I had brought along. "Does anyone have this book?" I would ask when I was done. If they did not, I would give it to them. One lady brought me a Filipino woven basket as a gift because I gave her a book. A couple of times we prayed over all the clinic's papers that showed the names of people needing physical help. Sometimes I would mention different ways of praying, such as spontaneous sentence prayers, two people to pray over the meetings, three people to pray over Jan, and so on. They always nodded and said a few words in English, indicating they understood. Then when we prayed around the circle, they prayed in their own language instead of English. So I had no clue whether or not they were following my directions.

One night as I walked back to the hotel with some of our group, I was silently praying. *Lord, I don't understand my prayer group. They are speaking in their language, and it's just not fair. They are praying around in a circle, and I can't understand a single word they are saying. You have to help me! Wait a minute. That's it. When I began the prayer group in Women's Ministries, there was one person I couldn't understand because I heard her in a foreign language. Then, because I asked, You turned it off. You can do anything! Now I want to hear this group in my language. Turn their language into English, so I can understand them.*

The next night I had forgotten all about my prayer and began explaining what we needed to pray for and how. As we went around in a circle, I felt more drawn in this time. As specific things were mentioned, I heard myself saying in response to several people, "Amen, yes that's right. Yes, Lord." As the last person prayed, it finally dawned on me that I heard all of them in English. I understood every word!

It was hard to sleep and wait till breakfast. The next morning, at breakfast, I asked my fellow mission participant, "Harriet, what did you think of our little prayer group?"

"Oh, I liked it; it was very nice," she responded.

"Could you understand them when they prayed?" I asked. She looked at me, questioning why I would ask that, and replied, "No, they spoke in their language." Once again a reminder that God is great, and He willingly helps those who trust Him.

The Amas church

While our team gathered in the back of the church for a team meeting, one of our sponsors approached the group. "We would like to know how many preachers are in the group. Then next Sabbath we will divide you up in teams of two to preach in as many churches as possible," he said.

"Oh, God, you have got to help me!" These words suddenly came out of my mouth. I could not help it, and I suddenly felt small and very insignificant at that moment.

Corleen looked at me and said, "You can come with me; I'll be the one to preach."

I quickly learned that many things in the Philippines are done spur of the moment and whoever shows up is involved in the program. Sabbath arrived, and Corleen and I found our place in the Amas church. They had a prayer, a little talk, and then without warning asked Corleen to sing. She later told me, "As I was walking up to the platform, I said an emergency, 'Lord, what do You want me to sing?' 'How Great Thou Art' came to my mind."

Then the person up front said, "One of the visitors from America will now present a talk on witnessing." Since I knew Corleen was giving the sermon and had already sung, I thought I better do my part and handle this one. I leaned over to her and said, "Well, I'm not an impromptu speaker, but I'll give it a whirl."

"I'll pray for you," she responded. As I stood up to talk, I thought of Matthew 10:19, "Do not worry about what to say or how to say it."

"I didn't want to come to the Philippines." Yes, this was the first sentence out of my mouth. A witnessing talk started to form in my mind that I knew was the truth and would get the people's attention. Continuing with, "When I saw the brochure advertising that they needed people to come, I quickly held it up in the air and told God, 'Don't make me go!' You see, I wanted to get the first word in, and I did not think there was anything I could do. I do not claim to have any credentials such as pastor, doctor, et cetera, and I find this somewhat humorous because it lends credibility to my daily God-through-me mantra. I have God's credentials. I pray, and that is all I claim I can do. I begin my day by asking God for a double portion of His Holy Spirit's power to be in my words, my thoughts, my actions, my deeds. You can pray a similar prayer, and God will put you in the right place at the right time, just as He does for me. He will give you people to witness to, pray with, and encourage . . .'"

After Corleen's sermon, we walked a couple of houses down the street to lunch at an elder's home. "We would like you to attend a youth meeting now," his wife said as we were finishing. As we walked toward the church, she assigned us topics to present at the meeting. In America, we plan days in advance what the order of service will be; in doing so, we may lose some powerful Holy Spirit spontaneity.

As we sat there in the sultry heat, longing for ice cubes, wondering what was next, someone said, "Now we will share a favorite text." Just like that, people stood up and shared a text. Because I could see evidence of God helping me, I shared Isaiah 41:13:

"For I am the LORD your God
   who takes hold of your right hand
and says to you, Do not fear;
   I will help you."

The people were a living, breathing example to me of what it must have been like in Christ's time. They extended church all day long—sitting at the feet of Jesus—listening, caring, fellowshiping with one another, and reciting texts for the sheer joy of hearing promises and each other. Not minding if anyone made a mistake, not caring if someone's presentation was perfectly thought out, perfectly presented, or went overly long. The most important thing was to share your testimony no matter what it is; the Holy Spirit does the rest. I was moved and strengthened by their energy. They reminded me of the disciple Matthew, who, upon hearing Christ's words "Follow me" (Matthew 9:9), immediately left his vocation. That very day he "e-mailed" his friends, coordinated a dinner party at his house, and put his new evangelism skills to work. Credentials or not, to me it was important to be there mingling with the people, praying with them and for them. Personally, I cannot think of a better witnessing strategy than "pray and mingle."

I want to pass out Scriptures!

Both Corleen and I wanted to give Bible studies in the Philippines and knew we were not going to get the opportunity, so we prayed about it. One day after breakfast I went outside to stretch my legs and eyed Romulo's motorcycle. The more I stared at it, the more I wanted to ride it. Soon everyone came out, and I approached Elmo (the pastor of the Kidapawan City church) and asked, "May Corleen and I borrow Romulo's motorcycle to ride?" (Romulo, our guide, was not there to ask.)

He could not seem to think of a reason why not and said, "Sure."

"I have a motorcycle license in my state of Oregon," I assured him, but he did not look worried. Corleen jumped on behind me, and we took off. She thought we were just going up the road; but as I went up the road, my mind began thinking about all the little scripture books we wanted to give out.

"Are you turning around here?" Corleen asked me when we arrived at the end of the road.

"Corleen, we could pass out the little scripture books we have left over. Don't you think that would be fun?" I asked. We dashed by the hotel and picked them up and said a prayer for God to put the right people in our path. Several miles later, in the middle of downtown, we jumped off, patrolled the streets, and passed out little books to anyone that looked interested. After congratulating ourselves on several successes, I jumped back on the motorcycle and began to kick-start it. *Jump. Jump. Jump.* Nothing! Just as I was wondering what I was doing wrong, a man started approaching us from across the street holding something in his hand. When the man stopped three feet away with his hand outstretched, I stepped closer to look at his hand and saw a little box of straight pins as he spoke words I could not understand. I thought to myself, *Oh, that's a relief; he is just trying to sell us something that looks like little pins.* I could not fathom what they were for and motioned that I was not interested and at the same time pulled out a book. I handed it to him and said, "A gift for you." He took it and studied it all the way back across the road, not watching for traffic. Of course, the motorcycle now started immediately.

Just when we thought "all is well"

"May these words of my mouth and this meditation of my heart be pleasing in your sight, LORD, my Rock and my Redeemer" (Psalm 19:14). This verse in Psalm 19 was written on the front of our daily prayer calendar, which Lois had made for us to give to the intercessors. Most mornings we would meet in the Whites' room for worship because they had the largest room. We wanted God to touch lives through our words and actions. We wanted God's strength to complete each task through us. We wanted to point to Christ as the Redeemer for His people. Daily we lifted up our requests and praises to God. Often when someone was feeling sick or frustrated, we noticed the person's name in the devotional for special prayer emphasis that day.

Before we left, I saw that it would be nine days before my name came up on the prayer list and then it was listed two days in a row. Lois had said, "I tried to put your name on other days but felt it should be listed back to back." On March 14, Shirley observed I was in pain; the next day I went to the hospital. God had directed Lois in placing those names. A few days prior, while riding in the van, I started holding on to my side. My side ached, and I could not figure out why. Had I injured a rib? I did not think so. Nevertheless, all day I clung to my side. Shirley looked at me and said, "You're telegraphing your pain to me." I did not know what she meant. So she questioned me further, "Are you having gallbladder trouble?" Not being a medical person I did not make the connection that a gallbladder could hurt in the spot I was holding. "You need to get that checked out because it could be serious," Shirley said.

"I'm going to think and pray about it first," I responded. This was rather sudden information for me. Back in our room, Corleen put her hand on my side and lifted me up in prayer that God would heal me. But God had other plans. Sometimes God uses our pain instead of healing us. While I was pondering my situation, Shirley called and reached a nurse named Shillah who had helped us at the clinic and worked at the Kidapawan Medical Specialist Center and arranged a time for me to go to the hospital. It felt like the devil was attacking me from the inside, trying to get me to go home. Kneeling by my bed, I poured my heart out to God. "Lord, You led me here. I know You don't want me to leave. I'm supposed to be here. I'm praying with many people here. Please help me." As I poured out my heart to the Lord, tears came to my eyes at the thought of leaving these precious people. After a time, peace began to wash over me, and I knew that no matter what happened, God wanted me to stay.

It made me feel better that Corleen, who by now had become my dearest friend as well as prayer partner, and Griffith and Shirley were going with me to the hospital. Griffith, a radiologist, planned to read the ultrasound. The ultrasound cost 450 *pesos,* which was a lot of money to Filipinos, but at the exchange rate of 40 *pesos* to 1 dollar, it came to $11.25. The diagnosis? No stones, or Shirley would have highly recommended I leave for America, but I had sludge in the gallbladder.

God "through" my gallbladder

God always brings blessings out of calamity, and soon my gallbladder problem began to open doors. On the way to the city of General Santos, Corleen and I had Romulo's ear the whole way because we sat up front where it was less bumpy. This seemed to be planned by God. Romulo asked us many questions about prayer. "Did you invent the term *prayer coordinator* for this mission trip, or have you always had it?" he asked.

"Many people hold the title of prayer coordinator in America, and we conduct prayer conferences and have prayer partners also," Corleen replied. We spent hours in the van talking with him before stopping for a couple of baptisms and a nice lunch. Along the way, we toured through areas where Romulo said, "Ten years ago Christians couldn't even travel through this Muslim area, or they would have been killed."

The Southern Mindanao Mission

Wendell Serrano, the president of the Southern Mindanao Mission greeted us in his office. It was here we told him that we had very special news for him. "Pastor Serrano, our team recently voted to give our remaining funds to the mission." He was elated as I counted out thirty-five hundred dollars to him in front of their treasurer, a secretary, Romulo, Jan, and Corleen, with the promise of two thousand dollars later. With these funds, they would be able to roof and order pews for five new churches, have ten of the Bible workers continue for a year, and provide Bibles for the 433 newly baptized members.

Earlier in our mission trip, there was a church member who donated two lots to be used to build one of the churches. We were able to have a dedication ceremony, complete with ceremonial ground breaking, songs, and an encouraging talk by Corleen. It blessed us tremendously to see our funds used in this way. What a fulfilling experience at the Southern Mindanao Mission in General Santos! After another three hours back in the van on bumpy roads to our hotel in Kidapawan City, I knew I could not handle another long ride, or even a short one. I needed to lie down. The pain had taken its toll. But I was determined to stay.

Moments of Reflection:

1. Are you determined to stay on the mission God is giving you?

2. Is everything fine in your life? Are you praying prayers of protection for yourself and others?

3. In what ways are you staying on guard against the evil one?

CHAPTER TEN

Mercy in a Jail

"I am there in the midst of them."
—*Matthew 18:20, NKJV*

These vehicles are huge," I said to Corleen early Friday morning as we strolled up to a big, red jeepney parked in front of the church for our team. Our sponsors thought it would be nice for us to ride Filipino style up to Mount Apo.

It was obvious that the owners took pride in dressing up their vehicles. As Corleen and I were walking toward the jeepney, I shared, "I really wish I could go with you. My gallbladder just wouldn't make it through another long, bumpy day though. I'm going to miss you. Pray for me that I will 'move only in the Spirit.' Maybe it is providential that I stay, and something interesting will happen."

"I will never cease to pray for you, my friend. I'll miss you too," she responded. With that, she climbed up to the front of the jeepney and stood on the very top of it with some of the others who were eager to try out riding on top like the locals.

I hitched a ride with our driver, Antoy, back to the hotel and said to him as I stepped out of the van, "Thank you for the ride. Would you please bring me some water? I turned in our jug that was empty this morning." He promised to bring me some.

Staring at the ceiling now while reclining on the bed, I thought, *It's going to be a long day here all by myself.* The whole team *and* all the sponsors were on the trip to Mount Apo. I cheered myself with the thought that I would spend some of the time praying and reading, and I planned to enjoy it. Then I would pack everything that could be packed because we were leaving in two days, and I dislike saving things for the last minute. *What will I do the rest of the time?* I wondered. Suddenly, I chuckled as I remembered a story.

One evening I "scared" myself while going over my before-bedtime mental checklist: put the Bible on the little table; look at tomorrow's to-do list; set out necessary items; take off my money belt. Money belt? Where's my money belt? My mind raced as I visualized the day's events. When I recalled my prayer group before the meeting, I remembered setting down my bag beside me. A few days earlier I put my money belt in my bag instead of strapping it to my body because the heat caused a rash. The prayer time was the only time I let go of my bag. It was always attached to me like an article of clothing because I carried important records in it. It really was quite heavy, and it made my shoulders ache. If someone stole it during prayer, I was going to be very upset. Was it in my bag? I could not picture it, but where else would it be?

My mind really raced. *My passport was in the bag. I'm not getting out of the country. The money! I've lost some of our money. I'm not getting out of the country.* This worried me the most. My mind suddenly went into overdrive, and I started to panic. I paced frantically. I shouted, "God, You know where it is! You've got to help me! Tell me where it is!" By this time, I was in full panic. God did not respond, so I started for the door, thinking, *I need Corleen.* Midway through our small room, God spoke, *"It's in your pillowcase."* I gasped, turned around, grabbed my pillow, and found it. My passport was there, my driver's license, and all the money except for two hundred dollars. I fell back on the bed with my hands above my head, drained of energy. A few moments later I leaned forward with my head in my hands because I still felt shaky. At that instant, Corleen and Sharon came into the room. "What's wrong?" Sharon's expression changed when she saw me. I could not answer right away; words would not come.

I was not the only one with money-belt issues. Three others had accidentally left their money belts in their rooms on various occasions and had money stolen. Phil and Jan reported our stolen amounts to the hotel manager. We did some serious praying. I could not sleep that night and kept praying, "Lord, You know what happened. You know why all of us are missing funds and what happened to them. Please tell me. Please tell me. Please help me." He did not respond. So I clung to my daily theme: "Lord, I trust in You with all my heart. And I lean not on my own understanding. In all my ways I acknowledge You. And You shall direct my paths." It was the wonderful scripture promise from Proverbs 3:5 that I clung to now as I stayed in my room, alone with my God.

Never a dull moment

Now my thoughts were interrupted by a knock at the door. It was An-toy with my water. Instantly, I could tell something was wrong with it. I opened my mouth to say something, thought better of it, and simply said, "Thanks," then closed the door. I stared at the water jug. It wasn't sealed. All of our jugs of water had been sealed. I was pretty sure that he would not give me something that was bad, but I determined I would not drink it. A funny feeling swept over me, and I said out loud, "Lord, I'm not drinking that water, and when I can't take it anymore because I get thirsty, I will go downstairs and buy something to drink."

I knelt by my bed to pray. Twenty minutes later my watch alarm startled me by going off. *That's odd, I don't remember setting it.* "Lord, I'm going to assume You are telling me it's already time to go downstairs." I stepped down the stairs to the lobby and around the corner to their small four-foot-by-three-foot-wide fridge, chose some bottled water, and took it to the counter. "Oh, you're here! We thought everyone had left," the lobby clerk said. As I walked back up the stairs, I thought, *Something odd is going to happen to me.* I shuddered. Hurrying back to my reclining position on the bed, I just wanted to sip my water and rest my gallbladder.

The phone beside me rang. "The manager wants to talk to you!" It felt like they were shouting. Startled, I went to the door, but someone was already banging on it before I got there. *How did they beat me to the door? It's such a small room,* I wondered. Opening the door, I saw the manager and another man with an urgent look on his face. The manager exclaimed, "We have a suspect at the police department. I need you to come with me." He was holding up a copy of a one-hundred-dollar bill. "I need to know if any of your funds are in sequential order with this one." Thinking quickly, I took the copy from him and said, "Just a second, I'll be right back," and closed the door on him. Now behind the door I prayed, "Lord, You have to help me."

I had closed the door on the manager because I did not want him to see where I kept my money belt. Now I had other thoughts. *We gave most of our money to the mission yesterday* (except for the money to pay for the hotel and emergencies), *and the money didn't come in sequential order when we got it in the States. And he doesn't need to see my remaining money.*

Opening the door again, I said, "You know, we gave most of our money away yesterday to a mission, and when we received the money in the United States, it was not in sequential order. I will come with you though." First, we went to the jail where a man questioned me. Then we drove to a city hall–type building where an investigator took my statement. He said, "The money changer in town witnessed Cyrus, a room boy at the hotel, changing money starting on March 21 [a Tuesday], and we need your information. What is your name?" I gave my name. "What is your occupation?" *Why does everyone ask me this?* Corleen told me at the beginning of our trip, "You can tell people you are the assistant for Women's Ministries because it is pending that you will take over the job in April right after we get back." She told me this the day our sponsors asked our occupations, and I felt bad because I was unemployed. This is when I grabbed hold of the fact that I am a servant of God and nothing is more important than that.

"I want you to know no one witnessed Cyrus taking our money, and anyone can take money to a money changer." He asked other questions and then said, "The manager will take you to the Hall of Justice now where you will sign this."

I appeared before an attorney and sat in front of his desk. The hotel manager went back down the hall. "Has anyone showed you your statement?"

"No, I was brought straight here, and I would like to see it." He handed me the thinnest paper I had ever seen. It was an odd-sized, eight-and-a-half-by-thirteen-inch, onionskin paper. After reading it, I said, "Three of your statements need to be changed. None of us saw anyone steal our money, so I can't agree with the statement that Cyrus did this. The next statement I can't agree with either because even if a money changer witnessed him turning in money that does not prove that he took ours; he could have gotten it elsewhere. And I was not the one who reported the incident, Jan did."

He asked, "If I change the one statement to Jan's name and the other two statements to say, 'I was informed that,' in front of the statements, then would you sign?" Trusting this man and sensing peace from God, I signed the paper.

Stepping into the hotel manager's jeep, I thought, *If only Corleen could see me now! She thinks I'm in the hotel room lying down. God really used my gallbladder pain to put me in the right place at the right time. He knew what He was doing by not healing me.*

"I'll take you back to the hotel now," said the manager.

"Can you take me to the jail instead? I would like to visit Cyrus; but let's stop by the hotel first, I want to get him a book," I remarked.

God in the jail

Thankfully, I had a few scripture books left and grabbed two. *I'll give one to the manager also.* Arriving at the jail, the manager found the man we met before and remarked, "She would like to see Cyrus." This man opened a door and said, "His cell is the second one down on the right." Taking a few steps forward, I hesitated at the top of the stairs, feeling the narrowness of the walls. *Slam* went the door behind me as I shuddered. *Well, there's no turning back now.* Reaching the bottom, my eyes adjusted to the four dimly lit crude cells, two on the left and two on the right. Walking a few steps farther, I reached Cyrus's cell. He recognized me and started talking loudly, "Big problem, ma'am! I don't know why they have me in here. Please get me out. I didn't do anything. I didn't take any money. They kill people who go to jail!"

I was conscious that anything I said would be heard by all the men in the cells. It felt strange, having never been in a jail. It made me uncomfortable, especially in a foreign country. I tried not to think about the fact that the man in the cell behind me was close enough to reach out and grab me. I thought, *It's interesting, I haven't even said anything yet, and he has said that he doesn't know why he is here and that he didn't take any money.*

As he was continuing, his voice rose to yelling that I needed to help him. It occurred to me that I knew people who had been falsely accused of things they had not done. I had seen others framed. Here I was in a position to help sort this out. I thought of my Lord and Savior Jesus Christ who hung on a cross with trumped-up charges against Him. I knew I needed to get Cyrus to believe it would be my God who would help him, not me. Then the choleric side of my personality came out. I held up my hand and pointed at him because he was continuing to yell. "Cyrus, you need to listen to me carefully. I want you to know that I personally don't accuse you of anything. I didn't see you do anything; only our God knows who did. He knows exactly what happened. He knows who took our money, whether it was you or someone else. And our God is here with us right now, and He is the only One who can save you and get you out of here. Here's a scripture book I brought for you to read. You apparently have lots of time to read. This book will lead you to a loving Savior, and you should accept Him as your Savior. Then no matter what happens, whether you get out of here or not, you will have eternal life." He softened and said calmly, "Oh, yes, ma'am, I will. I will read it. Thank you."

"Would you like me to say a prayer with you?" I asked.

"Yes," Cyrus responded.

Anything but a relaxing day

Shortly after 11:00 A.M., I was back in my room, reclining on the bed again when I heard another knock. *And I thought I would be bored today.* It was Christine, a hotel worker. "The manager sent you mango ice cream," she said. *Probably in thanks for my scripture book gift,* I thought. *Everyone here seems to want to give a gift in return. I like this country.*

"May I ask you a question, ma'am?" asked Christine.

"Of course," I replied.

"Did you ever give Cyrus any money?" she asked timidly.

"No," I responded and knew she was concerned for her friend Cyrus.

"Well, ma'am, did Corleen ever give him any?" she asked. I figured I knew Corleen had not but knew enough not to respond for her and said, "You'll need to ask her; I'm not sure." She looked worried and looked like she wanted to ask me another question, thought better of it, and turned away. Christine had been attending our meetings, was receptive to Bible truth, and had grown fond of our team.

Reclining on my bed again, I prayed, "Lord, please help me with this situation. I don't want to leave here without feeling this is resolved, and at the moment, it isn't. Also, would You bring me my corrected copy of my statement from the jail?"

At 12:10 P.M., there was another knock at my door. "Thank You, Lord," I said as I closed the door after receiving my corrected copy. I returned to my bed and thought, *I better write all this down. It will make a great story someday.* Shortly after that, in walked Corleen. "I kept thinking about you here all alone in your room, how did it . . . ?" She did not finish her sentence as she noticed I was busily writing, then looked at the empty mango ice-cream dish (I was still in shock and denial about what I should not eat with gallbladder pain). "I have a story," I replied. She sat down, and I shared the story.

Corleen joined me in the effort to pray that God's will be done and that the truth would come out about Cyrus. Corleen received a phone call from Cyrus's mother, pleading with her to do something. Corleen and I received a letter from Cyrus himself after Corleen paid him a visit that afternoon. "Dearest Madam Corleen and Diane, greetings to you. . . . I am one of your new inspired Christians through your Christian life. Thank you very much for the two hymnals that you have given to me [one day while cleaning our room he told us he wanted to be a singer]. I promise to the Lord to dedicate my life for Him through singing for His glory, it's a time also I encounter this kind of problem, which I could hardly bear it. I was accused of a sin which I am not guilty at all. . . . So please, madam, help me. As you know madam, many people bound to prison, who are not guilty at all." And his letter went on.

Wrapping up the loose ends

Our last day seemed packed with more activities than usual: Sabbath School, church, lunch, and a beautiful baptism by the river, with over one hundred baptized that day. Then we went to an Adventist chapel in a jail where Jan gave a talk, and we witnessed five people baptized in a water trough. From there, we went to a closing ceremony in the church. They bestowed little plaques upon us and many, many thanks. Then part of the group attended an anointing service for two ladies; one had a brain tumor, and one had breast cancer.

Back at the hotel, a man rushed me into the manager's office and closed the door. The manager put new papers down in front of me and said, "Just a small formality; please sign."

"Would you allow me to take these papers to my room to read and bring them back?" I asked.

"No, only a formality; you sign here."

"I'm sorry, but I'm going to need to read them first; I will bring them back," I urged and then went to my room. My heart sank as I read the papers. Similar to the first paper, they wanted me to sign that Cyrus had stolen the money. He may have been guilty, but no one had proof and I knew I could not sign. I prayed, "God, help me." Then I heard a commotion downstairs as our van pulled up.

I ran down to see Jan and Corleen and shared the latest. Corleen insisted, "I think we should go to the jail." I apparently did not hear her because I could only think about the hotel wanting me to sign the papers. Jan had an appointment she must prepare for, leaving Corleen and me to ponder the situation. We did not know what to do. I said I wanted to make a copy of the papers before deciding, and she felt like she needed to go to the gymnasium for the final evening's celebration. We prayed, and she left for the celebration. I sat immobile, not feeling compelled to leave the room.

Resolution in the jail

As soon as the door closed, the Holy Spirit prayed through me, "Oh, God, I need her help; please send her back." Suddenly feeling hungry, I turned around to my suitcase, reached in, pulled out a small, unopened package of Oreos we got three weeks earlier on the flight, and took a bite. At that exact moment, Corleen opened the door and entered the room, stating, "I left my water bottle behind," grabbed it, and walked out the door. It all happened so suddenly, as if in answer to my prayer, and I was still chewing and could not say anything.

When my mouth was clear, I heard myself pray those words again, "Oh God, I need her help, please send her back."

Unfazed by Corleen's previous entrance, I reached into the Oreo package and stuck another cookie in my mouth, soon followed by a third. The door opened, and in walked Corleen again. This time she grabbed a book. My mouth was full so, again, I could not say anything, and she walked back out the door. Suddenly, I grasped that God was doing something. "Lord, send her back a third time. Apparently, You think I need her." This time I did not chew anything and waited expectantly by the door for it to open again. Sure enough, Corleen came in moments later, and I said, "This is the third time I prayed that God would send you back."

She replied, "I was clear in the back of the van when I had this sudden urge to come back. I even had to climb over several people."

"I don't know why you're here, and I still don't know what to do about these papers," I replied.

With that, we knelt by my bed. After all the countless times we had prayed together on this trip, we knew well the impact of the Bible verse, "For where two or three are gathered together in My name, I am there in the midst of them" (Matthew 18:20, NKJV).

Like Daniel, we just started thanking our God for everything (Daniel 2:23). I began with the first thing that happened that day. Many minutes later I got to the part about the jail where Jan preached earlier that day. Then it came to me, and I jumped up and said, "That's it. That's it. It's the jail! We need to go to the jail!"

"I said that before," remarked Corleen.

"You did?" I asked, surprised.

"Yes, you were too distracted to hear," Corleen said.

"I'm sorry, but now it makes sense to me," I replied. We did not know what would happen, and we did not want anyone to prevent us from going—especially the manager who seemed anxious to throw the book at Cyrus. The jail that Cyrus was being held in was only a block and a half away. We set out in the darkness and soon entered the jail. Very quickly we found the investigator I had seen the day before, and he motioned us to sit by his desk. I held out the papers the hotel manager gave me and explained that I had not seen Cyrus take the money. I explained everything, including that our money did not come sequentially when we brought it. With the language barrier, he did not seem to understand, so Corleen started to explain using a few different words. His appearance began to change as if a little lightbulb came on. He took the papers and said, "I'll handle it from here, you don't need to sign these, and I'll notify the manager that I have the papers."

Finally, I felt peace about it and though we did not know what would happen to Cyrus, we knew we had done the right thing. Real people can be hurt by our actions, and it is best to stand up for truth.

My "daughter" Rochelle

Corleen and I walked to the gym for a game night hosted by our sponsors. My child friend Rochelle saw me and ran over to hold my hand. She pulled me over to a woman I assumed was her mother. Her mother apparently knew who I was and burst into tears. I do not know if she thought I was taking her daughter away or if she was grateful for all the things I had given Rochelle: a Bible, toys, bags of durian tarts (a fruit pastry), and much more. Her mother did not understand English. So I smiled, hugged her, assured her she had a lovely daughter and could keep her, finally said Goodbye, and turned away because I felt so bad that she kept sobbing and sobbing.

Rochelle then took me to her father, who surprised me by speaking English. He gave me their home address; over the years, Ron and I sponsored their children's educations. Now that Rochelle speaks English, we correspond via e-mail and look forward to her visit after she completes college. She calls Ron and I Daddy and Mommy. Through her, God gave me a child from the Philippines.

Did God reach many people through our team? Absolutely!

Moments of Reflection:

1. Share with your group or journal about a time when you suffered from an ailment. As you look back, how did God bring you through that experience? If you are still suffering, share how you are coping.

2. Read Matthew 18:15–35. Have you ever experienced the injustice of people assuming you were guilty of something when you were not? Have you asked forgiveness for assuming someone was guilty and later found out he or she was not? Journal or share any thoughts about Matthew 18.

CHAPTER ELEVEN

Sometimes Falling Down Can Be a Blessing

Do not neglect your gift.

—1 Timothy 4:14

L ife with God is rarely vague, and He faithfully led me toward the new job in women's ministries. This missionlike job was about to become more than I ever imagined.

One Sunday night, as I pondered our Monday morning prayer group, the thought came to me, *Sometimes it feels like we rush into requests; maybe God wants a moment to share something first.* "Lord, please help me to express my thoughts about this tomorrow," I prayed. Monday morning in our prayer group, the ladies began sharing prayer requests, and I fought a battle in my mind. *Should I say something? Maybe I won't.* The Holy Spirit kept nudging me, so finally I said, "We always jump right into prayer after we make a note of all the requests. Could we have a moment of silence first? In case God wants to say something," I urged. You should have seen the look on all three of their faces. *They don't know what to say,* I thought. There was a long pause, and then Corleen asked, "What do you want to do?"

"I don't know," I said. "It just feels like we are always talking and maybe God wants to say something to us."

It still felt like an awkward moment in the room. No one was sure what to do with my statement. Beth offered, "I'll begin." Three of us prayed just like we did every time we met. *Oh no, nothing new is going to happen, and I was too afraid to call for a moment of silence while I prayed.* Then Corleen began, "Lord, we want to take a moment of silence now to invite the Holy Spirit in." And all went quiet, very quiet.

Do not be afraid to make your *God-compelled* needs known. At that moment, our God sent in the powerful Holy Spirit's presence like we had *never* felt before. We all felt it. Corleen could hardly finish her words after that.

And I had tears in my eyes. It was powerful!

More God moments

New opportunities for speaking suddenly appeared on my horizon. Ginny Allen and Ione Richardson asked me to take twenty minutes of their seminar on prayer at the upcoming October 6–8, 2000, annual Christian women's retreat. Corleen asked me to share on prayer in a seminar at another venue. This desire to share what God was doing became exciting and worrisome. *How can I be a great speaker?* I wondered. I was trying not to compare myself with others who seemed so good at speaking. Putting down my thoughts on paper was the easy part. *How do I get it organized, back up my points, and make it interesting?* I wondered.

Trying to relax

One weekend Ron and I were able to go with Corleen and Lois and their spouses to central Oregon for fun and relaxation. *This will be a good way to get my prayer partners better acquainted with each other,* I thought. The weather was great, and we had a wonderful time walking, biking, talking, and praying.

On Saturday evening, I was showing Lois and Corleen my prayer partner talk, when I began feeling rather inadequate to the task. Corleen and I stayed up talking after the others had gone to bed. "I'm worried," I said. I was having a melancholy moment; but I have noticed that God can use these moments to intervene in a special way.

"Why are you worried?" she asked.

"Well, there is the talk you want me to do for your seminar in Bend. Then the one at the retreat," and I rambled on about nonsensical things. I really appreciate Corleen because she listens to me. Then she reminds me that I really do not have to worry. She said, "You'll do fine. God is helping you; you know that yourself. He has given you illustrations to use." Inevitably she gave up and said, "Why don't we pray about this? And give your burden over to God."

She said a nice prayer; but I still felt restless and later strolled outside by myself. Raising my hands and head to heaven, I pleaded, "Lord, You have to help me. Yes, yes, I know You have already. But I need help again. I want to be a better speaker." It was a beautiful evening. It often is in Sunriver, Oregon. Myriads of stars stared back at me and caused me to pause. "Lord, I'm in awe! What an incredible evening! You are truly the One who created this universe. You did such a great job. You can do *anything*." Remembering my original reason for standing outside, I pointed at the sky and added emphatically, "Now please help me with my speaking!" I turned and went inside the house.

Sometimes falling down can be a blessing

"We could probably fit in one more bike ride today," I encouraged the others on Sunday. Minutes later Lois said, "Don't you have a helmet?" I heard myself say, "I don't have to wear a helmet; I never fall off." *Oh no*, instantly I felt funny, as though something was going to happen to me. Brushing off the feeling, because I really enjoy bike riding, I stepped on the pedal to go, reasoning, *I really can't remember the last time I've fallen off. I must have been a child.*

Several miles in, we reached the Sunriver Nature Center, and our group was trying to decide which direction they wanted to go next. While they chatted, I started riding in a circle, then put my feet up on the handlebars, something I never do. Bored with that, I started to take my feet down, and they got caught. Suddenly, I felt myself falling. *"Aaaah!"* I exclaimed. *What happened?* I thought. It felt like I was falling forever. *Wham! Ouch! Ooooh!* I sighed. My bike was directly underneath me as I lay on top of it. *Did I break anything?* I wondered before I started to get up. Everything felt fine except for where the pedal was pressing into me. Looking over the damage, I realized the crankshaft was bent and could not do a full rotation now without hitting the frame, only a half rotation was possible.

"Do you need me to ride back with you?" Corleen asked.

"No, no, I'll be fine. You go ahead and enjoy the rest of the bike ride with the others," I replied. It took double the time to ride back by pedaling a half revolution forward then swinging the pedal backward and starting over. I had several miles to think by myself. "Lord, I'm sure You think this is funny," I said out loud. "I'm not sure what purpose it serves, but I want to thank You for cradling my fall. I praise You that I didn't break anything."

That evening my backside started to ache. "Would you make me something to eat while I just lie here on the couch?" I asked Ron. He started puttering about the kitchen, and I turned my head toward the coffee table. *Hey, that's right, I haven't read this book in months,* I thought. *I remember really enjoying it.* Grabbing the book *Silver Boxes,* by Florence Littauer, the memory came back of an Aspire Women's Conference I attended one May. I had met Florence in person. The book I held was personally signed; I remembered when she handed it to me that I had the feeling I would meet Florence again, but I wasn't quite able to grasp how that could happen. Opening the book to where I had left the bookmark, I read, "It was in the fall of 1980 that the Lord used one of Paul's encouraging statements to Timothy to start me on a ministry of encouragement to others. . . . I had gone from teaching Bible studies and giving my testimony at Christian Women's Clubs." *Hey, that's what I'm doing,* I thought. *I'm giving my testimony at a Christian women's retreat.* "There had been no mentor showing me what steps to take, and I had to learn the hard way, through experience." *I'm so lucky. I have a mentor named Corleen,* I thought amusedly. *This is a great book. I'm really enjoying this.* "Finally, all my years of work were bearing fruit, and I felt the Lord calling me to share what I'd learned with beginning speakers and potential writers." Florence had my full attention now. *Did I not just tell the Lord about my speaking needs?* I thought in awe. "I was committed to forge ahead and write what became CLASS, Christian Leaders and Speakers Seminars."[1]

Slam went the book on the coffee table. "That's it! That's it!" I exclaimed to no one in particular and leaped off the couch, ignoring my pain. "God wants me to go to a CLASSeminar!" I shouted. Getting on the Internet, I typed in a search string for CLASSeminar and realized falling off my bike had been a God-moment blessing.

CLASSeminar

The Internet revealed a CLASSeminar taking place on September 25–27, in Orlando, Florida. "Ron, I'm going to Orlando, Florida!" I shouted, not giving him a choice in the matter. Since I have given God my time and talents, my poor husband never knows what adventure God is taking me on next.

The next day, Monday, I called CLASSservices that ran CLASSeminars and learned they now had a longer name than the one in Florence's book. They had added the word *authors.* It was now Christian Leaders, Authors, and Speakers Seminar. "Yes, we still have spots open in our Orlando CLASSeminar. You're coming all the way from Oregon? That's great!" they said.

I called Alaska Airlines to get on a flight using my mileage plan. "No spots open in coach," they said. "There is one seat in first class using our TWA partner, and you have enough miles for it."

"I'll take it," I said.

Hanging up, I exclaimed, "Thank You, Lord, You just gave me a free flight to Florida. And You held that spot just for me."

I have never been so eager to go to something. I was sure the CLASSeminar was God's answer to help me speak and write better.

Mystery roommate

As soon as I got the listing of hotels in the area from CLASServices, I called the one they recommended. "Would you like a room with a king bed or two doubles?" they asked. I hesitated. "A king bed is fine, thanks," I replied. Why had I hesitated? I called Lois and told her the whole story. She helped me realize, from past experience, that if I have an odd feeling, it usually means a God moment. I called the hotel back. "I need to change from one bed to two; I'll have a roommate," I said confidently, even though I had no clue what I was talking about. Lois and my prayer group joined me in prayers for the CLASSeminar and my mystery roommate.

Preparing for the CLASSeminar

CLASServices sent assignments to be completed before I arrived. There were tapes to listen to and a personality profile to fill out; here, I confirmed that my personality is choleric and melancholic.

Two weeks and a day later my husband took me to the airport to fly to the CLASSeminar in Orlando, Florida. I still wondered about the mystery roommate.

CLASSeminar changed my life

"You're from Boring, Oregon?" a lady asked incredulously as she approached me. Wrapping her arms around me as though she had known me all her life, obviously a sanguine, she said, "I want to take you home with me after the CLASSeminar and show you the coast. You need to see the coast. Do you have extra days you can stay?"

"I'm sure that would be wonderful, and I wish I could. Thank you, but I have to leave early Thursday morning," I responded.

We all found a seat, and soon I heard Marita Littauer say, "Is there anyone here who needs a place to stay?" Many raised their hands. "Is there anyone who has room for someone to stay with them?" she continued. My hand went up. "OK, now I want you to get in contact with each other afterward."

On a break later, I walked up to one of the people needing a room. "Do you still need a place to stay?" I asked.

"Yes, thank you. I only need it Wednesday night though. The people I'm staying with are leaving Wednesday. Will that work for you?" she answered.

"Yes, I'm not leaving until Thursday morning," I said.

"I'll be in touch with you then," she said and walked off.

I was left to wonder, *What was so important about this?*

Each evening my head throbbed from all the information. One tip that Marita shared has changed my life. She said, "When you do a presentation, try to memorize all the scriptures you are going to use in it." Because an "authority figure" said it, my mind understood it like it was a given, that I must do it. Now fourteen years later hundreds of scriptures are in my head. Another very important fact I learned was that in every talk you need a point. "These points stick out of the water like a PIER," Marita said. PIER is an acronym for point, instruction, example, reference. For every point you express, you need to back it up with examples that come from your own experience, biblical examples, other people, and so on. These stories are what give your message life. Then you need references such as facts that authenticate your message. These can be from Scripture, books, statistics, magazine articles, and various sources. Your instruction is your "how-to" of what you want them to do as a result of your point. If you share all of these elements for every point, then for a thirty-minute talk to be effective, you will want three to six points. More could be written about this fascinating three days of learning. Little did I know what would evolve from this adventure in Florida. If we use what God gives us, it becomes a blessing for us and others.

Small-group blessing

When you attend a CLASSeminar, you will be asked to do four impromptu speeches. Everyone speaks to their own assigned small group. My small group had nine other attendees plus the leader, Georgia Shaffer, an author, speaker, and licensed psychologist from Pennsylvania. I was impressed by what she had shared up front in the general sessions, and now she did a good job directing our small group. "Lord, please help me," I prayed in my head before my speeches. The third day of small group was different from the others in that Georgia took us one by one out of the room and gave us helpful tips while the rest of the group filled out an evaluation on us.

"Diane, I noticed you are really good at coming up with these quips like 'God through me.' You should seriously consider turning your God-though-me idea into a book," she encouraged.

Sitting back in the small group, I offered up a prayer of thanks, and then God impressed me to pray that Georgia would be my friend. *Lord, this seems impossible. She lives on the East Coast, and I live on the West Coast.* But I prayed, "Lord, I like Georgia. I know this sounds improbable, but You can do anything.

I would like to see her again. Maybe become friends. Would You arrange that?"

Later I opened the card she had given me and it said, "1 Timothy 4:14, NIV, 'Do not neglect your gift.' "

Mystery solved

My mystery roommate appeared at lunch. "My friend and I have a car if you want to ride with us to the hotel, and I can unload my stuff," she said. "Let's meet outside after CLASSeminar ends." After taking the baggage to our room, she said, "My friend and I are going to a movie." She left, then got back very late. By Thursday morning, curiosity had almost killed me. "I just want you to know that I didn't originally have two beds." Her story spilled out, and it became clear as she explained, "God really wanted me to come to CLASSeminar. But I didn't have any money to pay for it. I wasn't going to come, and I told God that." She continued, "My friend who rented the car paid my way. Others pitched in for housing the other nights, and now I can see God's hand providing for the last night. Thank you so much."

"It's my pleasure. I was just letting God use me. May God bless you now through all you have learned in CLASSeminar," I said and hurried off for my early morning flight. I am learning to leave room for God to work. We do not know why He wants to do things a certain way, but He does want to work through us to touch others. He wants us to not neglect our "gift." I am convinced God *loves* to be involved in our lives. Sometimes falling down truly is a blessing.

Moments of Reflection:

1. Do you believe that what is happening in your life right now can be used by God? Are you praying to be an influence for Him?

2. Write down some ways the people in your life or your church are making a difference for God. Pray for greater influence, and claim John 15:7.

3. Find some verses you like and begin putting them to memory. Here is one helpful memorization tip: I prefer to memorize two verses a day while walking three miles. First, I recite one verse over and over while staring at the paper, using hand motions and overemphasizing some words for a full mile before working on the second verse. Mile three, I put the two verses together. May God bless you as you memorize.

---

1. Florence Littauer, *Silver Boxes: The Gift of Encouragement* (Dallas: Word Publishing, 1989), 98.

CHAPTER TWELVE

Testifying to the Good News of God's Grace

"However, I consider my life worth nothing to me; my only aim is to finish the race and complete the task the Lord Jesus has given me— the task of testifying to the good news of God's grace."

—*Acts 20:24*

Six months after returning from Florida, I was at the office one day when I felt compelled to see if I could visit Ione and pray with her on my way home.

"Yes, please come over," she responded on the phone. "I would enjoy praying with you."

Tearing myself away after prayer, I jumped into my car and backed out of her driveway while simultaneously reaching with my hand to turn on the radio. My desire for rock music had lessened since my college days to now and then listening to a soft rock station while in the car or eating lunch at home. But an earthly distraction, though small, is still a distraction from God's purpose. Just as soon as I touched the radio button, God "opened" my eyes. Outside of the car, I could see several demons fly up and attach themselves to the car as if going along for the ride. Horrified at what I saw, I quickly reached out again to turn off the station and thought, *Oh my! What an awful thing. I have to stop listening to this stuff!* If you think this is not happening behind the scenes, think again.

Two weeks went by, during which I apparently forgot the radio-in-the-car episode. One day while making lunch at home, I walked over to the radio station and just as I was lifting my hand to touch the dial, God said to me, *"The entire universe is watching you!"* I put my hand down and shuddered. *This is incredible. God is serious,* I thought. Another two weeks went by. Making lunch again, and out of habit, I walked over to the radio. Again, just as my hand went up to touch the radio dial, God said, *"The entire universe is watching you!"* My hand went down, and I said loudly, "That's it! Something is up with this!"

I walked over to my phone, called Lois, and told her about all three incidents.

Lois responded, "Diane, I have a story to tell you."

She has a story about this? I wondered.

She continued, "When we were at Sunriver, Ron and I were having a conversation. He shared, 'Diane is so close to God I don't know how she can listen to rock music. It just doesn't make sense.' So I thought, it's time for this to go in your life, and I said a prayer."

Surprised, I responded, "You said a prayer? One prayer? You never prayed about it again?"

Lois affirmed, "Yep, just one prayer."

"Well, that really shows the power of one prayer!" I exclaimed.

What about two prayers?

"Someone has been following me. Someone has been following me for the last month. I'm afraid for my life! Do you know what it's like to be followed?" These were the first words out of Kim's* mouth as she quickly walked up to my desk in the Women's Ministries office. She looked intently at me like she expected a reply, so I responded, "Yes, I have been followed." Apparently eager to know what happened, she jumped in, "Well, how did you get away from them? Did you pray?"

"No," I said, "I had the faster car."

As if pressing in with deeper concerns, she went on. "Do you believe that Christians are going to be persecuted in the last days?"

I was not sure where she was going with this statement, so I said, "Yes, and no."

"Well, do you believe I'm standing here in front of you?" she asked.

"Yes, I do," I replied. All the while I was thinking, *She clearly looks shaken.* "Let's go talk with Corleen," I added. Corleen and I listened but could tell Kim was a little apprehensive to tell us her whole story. She was homeless and penniless. The night before she had stayed at a friend's house, and her car had been stolen. She had just retrieved her car out of the impound lot before coming to see us. Looking pensive, she related, "Some people that I have to work with introduced me to friends of theirs, and they are worshipers of the devil. I was with them, and it scared me. They pray to the devil just

---

* Kim is a pseudonym.

like we pray to God, you know." She was sure they had taken her car, were following her, and her life was threatened. Then she stopped because she was hesitant that we would believe her.

"Kim, I have experienced some episodes from the community center that help me to know that what you are saying is very real. There is a great controversy between Jesus and Satan going on, and our God has already won the victory. He is with us, but the evil one is very mad. Shall we pray with you?" I asked. We prayed with Kim, then took her to lunch, and gave her some funds for groceries. Kim was attending Western Evangelical Seminary to attain a master's degree in counseling, and we could tell that God was working through her. After a few more conversations, a couple of weeks later we employed her as a stipend intern. She helped us get ready for some events, did some presentations, and went on visitations.

One day Corleen and I visited with a lady who was very depressed, and our visit did not seem to make much difference, so we sent Kim a few days later. Kim came back with an upbeat report. So I asked, "What did you do that we didn't?"

Kim responded, "You forgot about our health message. I shared that she needed to open the drapes and let the sunshine in, then handed her some water, and encouraged her to drink it, and take a short walk. Never underestimate the difference practical tips can make."

Tons of stories and prayers later, and all too soon Kim graduated and moved back to Texas. Then, in 2005, we received a call to come to her wedding. So in September of that year, Corleen and I flew to Dallas. While we were flying, I read from a *Discipleship* magazine and felt compelled to memorize a text I saw in it, especially the last part of it. It was Acts 20:24, "However, I consider my life worth nothing to me; my only aim is to finish the race and complete the task the Lord Jesus has given me—the task of testifying to the good news of God's grace."

The day before the wedding we had a wonderful time visiting with people at Kim's church. One lady was chatting with us and asked, "What do you like about Oregon?"

I replied, "We don't have any bugs."

Startled, she questioned, "You don't have any bugs in Oregon?"

Corleen jumped in, "We have bugs."

I countered with emphasis, "No, we don't have any bugs."

As if not hearing Corleen because of my emphasis, the lady looked surprised and replied, "That's amazing, no bugs," turned and walked off.

Corleen then gave me a look that said, *Why did you say that?*

"The fields here are so loud with bug sounds. I've never experienced bugs so loud! Oregon is so quiet, alas, no bugs," I said.

Another lady walked up to Corleen as I sauntered off. Olga asked, "What do you do with the women in Oregon?"

Corleen replied, "We do many programs for training them in ministering."

Olga replied, "What an interesting concept to train women. I never thought of that."

Helping with a wedding

We had mentioned to Kim that we wanted to be helpful. So after a delightful afternoon touring the farm where Kim and Dave* planned to live and spending time with them, we went to the rehearsal. It was here that Corleen and I learned for the first time that we were in charge of the reception cake and punch. I had never made specialty punch in large quantities for a wedding before, so we spent some time looking over the kitchen and the ingredients and then left for our lodging.

"Ministering like Jesus"

The ceremony was very nice, and we were so glad we were there to witness our friend's special event. We dashed to the reception and barely stayed ahead of people eating cake and drinking punch. After the church reception, we tidied up in preparation for the dinner reception, which was to include drinking and dancing. Because this was not an interest for us, we agreed that we would leave when the dance floor began to fill. Since Jesus also ministered by helping people at a wedding, I am sure God laughed at the thought of our leaving early. Our vegetarian plates were delicious, and we chatted with a few people on our side of the large round table.

An interviewer strolled by with a video camera, and we were able to share nice sentiments for Kim and Dave. Then everyone was invited to the dance floor. As people went to the dance floor, I looked at Corleen and asked, "Are we going to leave now?"

"Let's stay a little longer," she replied. She looked like she was searching for a reason to stay.

Why is she changing her mind? I wondered.

"Maybe we can discuss what we could put in the report about women's ministries," she finally said.

* Dave is a pseudonym.

94

I thought to myself, *OK, well, that's an odd thing to do, but maybe there is a reason for a delay.*

"We could choose a text that can work like an outline," I replied.

She pulled her Bible out of her purse and handed it to me.

At that moment, a man far across the table from us looked at me and, with a semiloud voice, asked, "Do you have a scripture for me?"

Holding the Bible in my hand but not opening it because the text I memorized on the plane suddenly came to me, I replied emphatically, "Yes I do, your text is Acts 20, verse 24, the last part, '[You have] the task of testifying to the good news of God's grace'!" It definitely pays to memorize Scripture.

Unexpectedly, the man suddenly stood, walked around to our side of the table, sat down next to me in a seat just vacated by someone heading to the dance floor, and said, "You have convinced me to become a vegetarian!" In my mind, I thought, *What? What just happened? How does this relate?*

We pressed in to hear over the loud rock music as he said, "I have been watching you and noticed that you ordered vegetarian. God has given me the spirit of discernment, and I know that you are godly women. God has pointed out others in the room that I have talked to and given encouragement to, but you have changed my life. You see, when I was twenty-four, I asked the Lord into my life; I did some awful things before that. And God has been showing me things to change ever since, and lately He has impressed me to become a vegetarian. So now because of you two, I am one. Now show me that text you told me." I opened the Bible, and he read it and exclaimed, "That's it! That is what I like to do. I like to tell people about Jesus." He proceeded to ask, "And what do you think about this text?" and then, "What do you think about this text?" We kept sharing the good news about Jesus.

Meanwhile the music seemed louder and louder. However, we remained focused on our new friend. He said, "I almost didn't come all the way from Arizona out here, but now I know God wanted me to meet you. Will you continue to pray for me?" We promised we would, and then we prayed with him right there. What an awesome thing, a life changed! Corleen and I stood up and ventured over to say Goodbye and hug Kim and Dave, then left to prepare for our return to Oregon the next day.

It is amazing that every time God's grace touches our lives, we have new ways to testify about it.

Moments of Reflection:

1. Did any issues come to your mind in the first part of the chapter that you wish to give over to the Lord? Pray, "Lord, I surrender this issue _____, and You are going to have to take it because I struggle to hand it over myself. I claim 2 Corinthians 10:5, 'We demolish arguments and every pretension that sets itself up against the knowledge of God, and we take captive every thought to make it obedient to Christ.' "

2. Journal about a time you testified to "the good news of God's grace," and then find a way to share the story. Or pray for an opportunity to testify to "the good news of God's grace."

CHAPTER THIRTEEN

Anyone Can Be of Service

"Your first duty is to begin by prayer. . . .
Hope for nothing from your own labors, from your own understanding:
trust solely in God, and the influence of His Spirit."[1]
—Martin Luther

One day I felt compelled to do my devotions in a park before heading into work. Opening to where I left off the previous day, I re-read one of my favorite stories—Elijah on Mount Carmel, in 1 Kings 18:36–38:

> "LORD, the God of Abraham, Isaac and Israel, let it be known today that you are God in Israel and that I am your servant and have done all these things at your command. Answer me, LORD, answer me, so these people will know that you, LORD, are God, and that you are turning their hearts back again."
>
> Then the fire of the LORD fell and burned up the sacrifice, the wood, the stones and the soil, and also licked up the water in the trench.

Imagine my surprise when I picked up the Christian magazine I had brought along and read through an article entitled "Seeking the Divine Fire." *This is not a coincidence,* I thought as I drove to the office.

Sometime in the afternoon I was relating the park experience to Corleen when her phone rang. "I'm not sure I can make it that weekend, let me ponder some names, and call you right back," I heard her say as she ended the conversation. Turning to me, she said, "A church in Pendleton wants a speaker for May 12. Should I give them your name?" My mind went back to my devotional time that morning, *Hmm, maybe God has just given me a title and theme for a talk called Seeking the Divine Fire.* Without even waiting for my response, because it seemed obvious God had chosen, she picked up the phone and called them back.

Planning begins with prayer

We began work on an event called God Through Me . . . Serving With Excellence, to encourage the average person in service for God. One Monday morning in our prayer group we lifted up petitions to God, specifically asking for a small planning committee to help and that the right speakers would be chosen for the event. Corleen typed up texts on a sheet that she thought fit with our theme, and we held them up to God for His wisdom. After praying, we started suggesting names; one was a lady named Clarissa. No sooner had we agreed on her than she walked around the corner, and we understood that God confirmed our choice. This training event was geared for the average person to know how events are formed behind the scenes, rather like a how-to event; such as how to make presentations, how to give Bible studies, how to tell children's stories, and how leaders do what they do so that work for God does not seem scary. Rather like a unique nuts-and-bolts conference with special demonstrations that equip people with answers. We say, "Lord, here I am, but could You have the professional do it instead?" Yet, God wants to develop the talents we already have, and He encourages us to use them in our current situations to glorify His name. Jesus mentored His disciples, then, empowered by the Holy Spirit, His disciples turned the world upside down. Jesus challenges us today, "Anyone who believes in me will do the same works I have done, and even greater works" (John 14:12, NLT).

Anyone can be a leader

One day we were discussing possible seminars. "There is a lady named Cheryl Hayton that has been giving Bible studies in her home for many years," Corleen remembered.

"Let's call her," I responded. "That's one of the topics we wish to present," but neither of us picked up the phone. Less than an hour later, Cheryl Hayton called *us* regarding a question she had about something totally different. I had never talked with Cheryl before in my life and now I said, "Cheryl, I'm so glad you called. We were just talking about you." In my mind, I was saying, *Thank You, Lord. This is a God moment.*

"But I'm not a leader," she said. "I've never taught about what I do; I just do it."

"That's precisely our point," I replied. "We want people to know that if you, an average person, can give Bible studies in your home, so can they. Don't worry. God will help you." After praying about it, she agreed to come. Another seminar we decided to have was called Steps to Sharing Jesus, to be presented by Carol Smith. Carol shared some of her tried-and-true tips:

1. Think about your own relationship with Jesus first, so you will know what you want to share with others.
2. Tell the truth to people, and let the Word of God speak for itself.
3. "How beautiful . . . are the feet of those who bring good news" (Isaiah 52:7). Keep your words simple, short, and sweet.

And so it went. All of our speakers and seminar presenters were chosen with what seemed to be God's blessing. Great things were happening. Oh, we still had a few program changes and some glitches, but in each one we saw God intervene.

Great idea, but I have something better

We needed some fun things to give away at our conference. Because I recently had such a wonderful experience at the CLASSeminar, I began to think about how beneficial it would be to promote them at our event. *Surely, it would be in their best interest to donate pens or something to us,* I thought. Corleen was not at the office, so I could not ask for her advice. *She would agree with me that we need pens; I'll call CLASServices,* I thought, convincing myself.

Picking up the phone, I pushed the numbers, "Hi, I'm Diane Pestes, and I was at the Florida CLASSeminar you had last year, and I'm calling from . . ."

"We were just talking about you," said Linda Jewell. This statement caught me off guard because I had not made contact with CLASServices since I went to the Orlando CLASSeminar the previous September. However, Linda was quick to say, "If we remember right, it was your Oregon Women's Ministries that sponsored CLASSeminar in Portland many years ago, right?"

"Yes, they did, and I heard it was very successful. People still talk about it," I replied.

"And you recently attended a CLASSeminar, didn't you?" Linda asked.

"Oh, yes, and I learned so much; it has changed my life," I responded.

"We were discussing that maybe you would like to sponsor us again," said Linda.

"I'm sure that would be wonderful! I'll have to ask Corleen though. What would we need to do?" I asked. Linda explained and offered to mail us the information.

They did not have any promotional pens, but God used that thought to get me to call them. This was exciting! I could not wait to tell Corleen. And it was April 10. I had been hired in Women's Ministries that exact date the previous year, right after coming back from the Philippines. The next day Corleen was in the office, and we began praying about bringing a CLASSeminar to Portland. It was not long before we confirmed the dates of April 8–10, 2002, to sponsor them, and we began planning for that as well as our other events. It is interesting that sometimes when you are in the middle of planning for something, God gives you something else to work on also. As if He is very excited.

Meanwhile, our God Through Me . . . Serving With Excellence nuts-and-bolts event was about to start. Corleen was going to give her testimony at the first meeting after some preliminaries. Two ladies, Connie Andrews and Jessie Curtis, from the Gladstone Seventh-day Adventist Church had graciously helped by organizing a prayer group that met during registration. Even though they covered our event in prayer, I still wanted to pray one more time with Corleen before her talk that evening. Finally, we had a quiet moment. "Our dear heavenly Father, here we are at Your event. Are You excited?" I asked in prayer. "Lord, my friend Corleen needs Your help tonight. Her throat is sore, and she needs You to speak through her."

Clarissa led the congregation in song. Then I gave a welcome. "Is there anyone else that can do the welcome instead of me? Surely this must be Corleen's talent or Cheryl's talent or Clarissa's, not mine." Looking skyward, I said, "Lord, here I am, but could You have the professional do it instead? How about Leslie? No?" Glancing back at the congregation, I asked, "Have you ever felt like this? Raise your hand if you have." Ninety percent of the audience raised their hand. "Then you're in the right place. All right then, Lord, we now decide to believe we can do anything with Your help." I prayed more, then spoke to the congregation, "Thank you for responding to the promptings of the Holy Spirit to bring you here. You all have a unique story. We don't want this to be just a mountaintop experience. We want you to take God back with you to your circles and communities of influence and share your own testimony of what God is doing through you. What a difference that will make!"

A few more special nuts-and-bolts items, some prayer time with the audience, and then Corleen took the stage. "In spite of the fact that I was so shy, God let me know through my parents, 'You are God's special child.' God has put me here on this earth for a special reason," she asserted. "I loved Jesus so much I wanted to share Him with everyone. But I was so scared." Corleen shared her unique, Spirit-filled story about how a school official told her a test revealed she should be a truck driver. She wanted to marry a pastor and sing in evangelistic meetings, and it happened, twice, then she said, "Now tell me God doesn't give you your heart's desires. He knows the plan He has for your life too. And the devil loves to try to put roadblocks in there to mess up God's plan. But let me tell you, if you keep hanging on, He'll carry you through. He will give you your heart's desire. There are people that I can never reach with God's love that you can reach because of your personality. The character traits God has given you—He needs all of us working together to accomplish *God through me.*"

"Anyone who believes in me will do the same works I have done, and even greater works" (John 14:12, NLT). Are you ready to step out in faith with the talents God has given you?

Moments of Reflection:

1. Do you always have your devotions with God in the same place? Think of ways you can add variety to your time with God.

2. Do you believe God wants to develop the talents you already have and use them in your current situation to glorify His name? List some of your talents you would like for God to use, and share them with your group or journal them.

---

1. Martin Luther, quoted in Brandon Merrick, "Pastor's Corner," Christ the Life.org, accessed October 21, 2014, http://www.christthelife.org/Devotions.html.

CHAPTER FOURTEEN

Seeking Healing

Heal me, LORD, and I will be healed; save me
and I will be saved, for you are the one I praise.
—Jeremiah 17:14

E ver notice how the devil throws in distractions when you are going on God's errands? Four days before I was to preach in Pendleton, my mother doubled over in pain and went to the emergency room. The day before I was supposed to speak in Pendleton, I awoke feeling sick. I drove to the hospital to be with my father while my mother was in surgery. My energy was just starting to wane when a doctor came out and said, "We've encountered a slight problem, and it will take another hour and a half." My mind started calculating. *It's going to be midnight before I get to my hotel if I wait till she's through surgery. I better just let my father tell her I had to leave.*

"Corleen, can you come with me to Pendleton? I don't feel very well, and my throat's very scratchy," I asked via my cell phone.

"I think I can get out of what I was going to do," she replied.

"Oh, good, I would feel better if you came. Can you meet me at my house in thirty minutes?" I asked.

"Yes; are you sure you want to leave your mom?" she asked.

"I know that God is in control," I replied. In faith, I left my dad in the waiting room with the unknown outcome.

Two hours later and an hour into our journey, I said, "Corleen, would you drive? I need to pull over. I don't have any more energy, and my neck is aching." When we reached our hotel in Pendleton, I barely managed to drag in my suitcase, paused for a look in the mirror at my throat, and saw several white dots had broken out amid red bumps in my already very red throat.

"Oh, no! Corleen, look! God, you have to help me! Corleen, we have to pray!" I exclaimed and knelt by the bed.

"Well, it's a good thing you brought an elder with you. I can anoint you," remarked Corleen. We prayed, and she anointed me. Then she got out her Bible, pulled up a chair by a table, and said, "Maybe you brought me because I might have to preach."

Reaching for the heating pad I had brought, I got in my bed, stuck it under my neck and sighed, "I know God wants me to do this," and fell asleep, exhausted.

The next morning I awoke and was surprised. *Hey! No pain!* I jumped up and looked in the mirror. "Look at that, no white dots, no red bumps. I'm healed! I'm healed!" I shouted.

Later, while sitting on the platform, I prayed for God's Holy Spirit, and as if in answer, it felt like the Holy Spirit was pouring into me. I can only preach if God gives me words to say. There is no reason to attempt it otherwise. I want to "speak as though *God* himself were speaking *through [me]*" (1 Peter 4:11, NLT; emphasis added).

My friend Julie was there and walked up with Corleen afterward. "Diane, I noted the presence of the Holy Spirit in the room." Many people said, "Thank you for your message on prayer," or "That was just what I needed." One older lady felt like God was not using her anymore, and it was a joy to pray with her.

Another moment of healing

A month later, on June 15, Corleen and I went to a camp meeting in southern Oregon. She was to present seminars titled "Contagious Christianity," and "Giving Your Testimony." God had impressed her with the importance of a personal testimony at our God Through Me event. Stopping for a bite to eat at Taco Bell on the way, Corleen stated, "I don't feel like eating," confiding, "I'm in a lot of pain. If this keeps up, I'll be visiting a doctor tomorrow, and you will have to give my seminar." Her description sounded like my mom's before she went to the emergency room with diverticulitis pain. Later that evening Corleen was feeling worse, so we knelt to pray some more.

Remembering my recent anointing, I said, "Corleen, maybe I should anoint you. Remember what happened to me in Pendleton last month."

"Yes, let's do that," she responded. We got out the oil, and I anointed Corleen.

As soon as I was awake the next morning, I could not stand the suspense. "How are you?" I asked.

"No pain! None! It went away last night," she replied.

"Again I say to you that if two of you agree on earth concerning anything that they ask, it will be done for them by My Father in heaven" (Matthew 18:19, NKJV). Praise the Lord! Amen.

Biblical anointing

The anointing idea used in our women's ministries originated several years ago at an annual Christian women's retreat. A woman approached Corleen about a friend who needed anointing. Corleen made several calls to people in the Oregon Conference Administration Department until finally reaching Clif Walter. Corleen explained she was trying to find a pastor who would conduct the service. Clif, a vice president of the Oregon Conference at the time, said, "You don't need anyone to come. You're a commissioned minister. You do it!" Since that day, hundreds have been anointed at Oregon Conference retreats. As many women elders are involved as possible to anoint the people who crowd the prayer room. Because people always have lots of questions and want to know scripture promises to claim, we compiled a handout with more information. Currently, it can be viewed on my Web site at www.dianepestes.com under "Resources."

Anointing is mentioned in both the Old Testament and New Testament. Kings and priests were anointed in the Old Testament as a symbol of the Holy Spirit coming upon them to lead God's people. In the New Testament, James expands the idea by inviting people to engage in this when they are sick. James 5:13–16 says,

> Is anyone among you in trouble? Let them pray. Is anyone happy? Let them sing songs of praise. Is anyone among you sick? Let them call the elders of the church to pray over them and anoint them with oil in the name of the Lord. And the prayer offered in faith will make the sick person well; the Lord will raise them up. If they have sinned, they will be forgiven. Therefore confess your sins to each other and pray for each other so that you may be healed. The prayer of a righteous person is powerful and effective.

The Bible invites us to pray whenever there is a need. We can prepare for anointing by asking God to prepare our hearts, asking for cleansing forgiveness from sin (1 John 1:9), and accepting the forgiveness. If someone feels like he or she cannot gain victory over a sin problem, this can be made a subject of prayer in the anointing service. Psalm 66:18 shares, "If I had cherished sin in my heart, the Lord would not have listened." Know that God wants you to have the victory. It is the devil who gives negative thoughts about our standing with Jesus. Other scriptures that can be studied include Psalm 103:1–6; 107:17–20; Mark 6:13; and 3 John 2. Corleen and I often tell people that God always heals in some way: whether it is physically, spiritually, emotionally, now or later through a physician's knowledge or when Jesus comes, He always heals. The most important point is to reach out to Jesus.

A perfect example of a woman reaching out is in Matthew 9:19–22:

> So Jesus and the disciples got up and went with [the synagogue leader]. Just then a woman who had suffered for twelve years with constant bleeding came up behind him. She touched the fringe of his robe, for she thought, "If I can just touch his robe, I will be healed."
>
> Jesus turned around, and when he saw her he said, "Daughter, be encouraged! Your faith has made you well." And the woman was healed at that moment" (NLT).

One of my favorite anointing memories is from a 2002 women's retreat. A lady came requesting emotional healing. Later she told Corleen that while she was being anointed she felt a warm hand on her side. She had been in a car accident in 1996 that broke a rib. It stuck out her side and was painful. Her rib was instantly healed and put back in place; the pain instantly gone. She said, "I guess the Lord knew I needed physical healing in order to have emotional healing."

Prayer Quest

In 2006, as I was leading out in an anointing service at an event called Prayer Quest, I shared the story about being healed during my first retreat. "Here's why it's biblical to anoint and a few helpful tips. . . . How many elders do we have here?" I asked. Nine people raised their hands. "Please come forward. How many people would like to be anointed?" About thirty raised their hands. I did not count them for lack of time. *Oh my! This is big*, I thought. To the elders, I encouraged, "People in your group who want to be anointed do not need to give a long explanation if they are uncomfortable. They can simply say it is a physical, spiritual, or emotional need. If they do give explanation, encourage others not to jump in and try to solve the problem. The person with the need may have people they bring with them to support them in prayer, so be sure to give them the opportunity. Also, at the end, it's a good idea to include praise in song or a thought for what God has done, and encourage them to continue to praise rather than revisit the problem." Turning to the larger group, "The elders will space themselves throughout the sanctuary, and you can follow them in groups of two or three with your supporting prayer people, and I also am an elder and will be over there," pointing toward the back.

As I started to walk away, two ladies came up to me. "Would you anoint me?" said the one lady. "Sure; let's go over to that pew," I said. Sharon introduced herself and related, "I could identify with your sinus problems and want to be healed from that and negative thoughts." I turned toward the other lady, "Are you here to support Sharon in prayer?" The other lady, named Donnie,* apparently did not hear my question or was thinking about her issues because she proceeded to tell me about her allergies. So then I knew she wanted to be anointed as well. She paused, looked at me hesitantly and continued, "I've never told anyone this before, but I also have hepatitis C." Then she looked doubtful and said, "But no one has ever been healed of that."

I thought, *No one should ever say, "No, it can't be done," because you never know what God wants to do.* A song came to mind, *My God is so great, so strong and so mighty! There's nothing my God cannot do.*

Instantly, God put the name *Cheri Peters* in my mind, so I said, "A lady named Cheri Peters has been healed of hepatitis C and has a powerful testimony, and God will give you a powerful testimony also. It is going to be unique, and it is going to be your own."

Just then the other lady between us spoke up excitedly, "Yes, that is true. I've seen Cheri Peters on 3ABN, and she was healed."

We had some prayer time, and "God through me" anointed both Sharon and then Donnie. Afterward Donnie said, "God did something! I know He did! I felt a warming!" Hugging them both, I wished them God's blessing and felt compelled to leave. Moving toward the other side of the sanctuary, another lady hurried toward me, grabbed my arm, and exclaimed, "We were so terrified, we were so terrified we couldn't move!"

"Huh?" I responded.

"When you said to disperse to a group, we were too terrified to move, and my mom and I just sat there. And my mom needs anointing. Can you find someone to anoint her?" the lady said.

"Where is your mother?"

"She is sitting in the pew," she responded.

* Donnie is a pseudonym.

"Does she want to go to a private spot?" I asked.

"No, I think she just wants to sit there," she said. As I approached, I noticed a cane beside her mother, and she looked to be around eighty. Sitting down, I looked up just in time to see her daughter was leaving us. I had assumed that her daughter would stay as prayer support.

I looked at the mother and asked, "Did you need your daughter here? Shall I get her?"

"No, just you will be enough."

Looking intently into her eyes, I asked, "What is your need?"

She repeated the same thing her daughter said, "I don't know; I just feel I need to be anointed."

I thought to myself, *Hmm, maybe reading something from the Bible might draw out a need.* To her, I said, "Well, God knows your need, and let's see what we can find out." My Bible fell open (sometimes it is as if angels turn the pages) to Psalm 94:19, "When anxiety was great within me, your consolation brought me joy."

"Yes, I am anxious," she replied. Turning to her, I shared, "Perhaps you are anxious because you know God wants to do something in your life, but you don't know what. God will give you joy." She seemed to relax some. After a little more discussion and because I knew God could guide her and give peace in her heart, I prayed over her and "God through me" anointed her. Again, I felt compelled to leave.

"For everyone who asks receives"

Rounding the corner in the lobby, I stopped by our information table. Approaching from the other direction was our speaker for the afternoon, Janet Page. Her first words were, "Please anoint me; I'm very sick." I knew she was our next main presenter and that this was not good. She continued, "I sat by Jerry all during the anointing as he anointed people, and I kept coughing and couldn't say anything. I'm not going to be able to speak next if God doesn't heal me, so will you anoint me?" She suddenly sat down in a chair, and I took the seat beside her, grabbed my Bible, and opened it. I claimed a scripture for her and prayed over her, particularly, that God would do for her like He has done for others, that when she stood up to speak she would be powerful and have no trouble. When I was done, I told Janet, "I'm going to sit on the front row, hold open my Bible, point to a verse, and share with the Lord that He needs to keep you free from coughing the whole time you are presenting."

We walked in and sat on the front row. Janet tried to stifle coughs and kept swallowing water. When she walked on to the stage, I held open the Bible, pointed to Isaiah 61:1–3, and told the Lord, "I'm claiming this for Janet. Please make sure that she is powerful, that she doesn't cough, that she doesn't need to drink her water, and that her throat is fine," I went on and on. This was being filmed, so I knew it was important for more than those in the room. When Janet was done and stepped off the stage, she started coughing again. I exclaimed to her, "God was so good!"

At her next presentation, she was coughing on the front row before she got up, and when she stood up to speak, I held open the Bible to Isaiah 61 again, tapped the verses I was claiming, and started praying again. Janet was powerful, and I could tell the people were spellbound and touched. All three presentations God did through Janet were touching, heartfelt, and a powerful blessing.

My God is great, so strong and so mighty! There's nothing our God cannot do. It happened just like the song.

There is such a need for prayer revival among God's people. And if they are burdened down with spiritual, physical, emotional, and other issues, then there is also a need for healing prayer and anointing among God's people. Jesus healed many people when He was here, and He still performs miracles. Not that He always answers in the way we hope, but He can if He wants to, and He urges us to ask. Luke 11:9, 10, beckons, "So I say to you: Ask and it will be given to you; seek and you will find; knock and the door will be opened to you. For everyone who asks receives; the one who seeks finds; and to the one who knocks, the door will be opened."

Moments of Reflection:

1. Have you ever been healed from a physical, emotional, or spiritual affliction? Journaling can be fun when you remember how God has blessed as you write notes about your experiences. Try starting now with one story at a time, or share with your group about a time you were healed.

2. If this chapter has awakened a desire for healing that you did not have before, then seek advice from a pastor or an elder at your church. Also look at the anointing information on my Web site, www.dianepestes.com, and make plans to follow through in reaching out to Jesus.

3. Have you ever asked for the Holy Spirit to anoint your words? Review Isaiah 61:1–3 and other verses on the Holy Spirit, such as Psalm 51:10–12; John 14:16, 17; and Acts 2:16–18. Spend some time praying over and pondering these and other verses you may find.

CHAPTER FIFTEEN

Are You Out of Work? You're Hired!

" 'Why have you been standing here all day long doing nothing?'
" 'Because no one has hired us,' they answered.
"He said to them, 'You also go and work in my vineyard.' "

—Matthew 20:6, 7

I n 2002, my brother was out of work. He said, "I feel helpless; I have the feeling that life is in disarray. It is bizarre to hear how companies just three years ago were begging for people to come to work. Now those same people wouldn't be able to find a job." He continued by saying, "The Internet reflects that those who are finding jobs are just moving from one company to another company."

This was a difficult time for our family. My brother Mark was also going through a divorce and had a three-year-old he took care of 90 percent of the time. The job loss occurred due to problems in the marriage. One day he was at my house for lunch, and I decided to pray a prayer of blessing over him as well as the food. Ten minutes later the phone rang. It was someone on the line for my brother with these words, "I accidentally hit your car."

What do you say to someone in this situation? Especially just after you prayed a prayer of blessing. It would not be appropriate to say, "Oh, it could be worse, I know four people right now who have brain tumors" (I did know them!). Or do you quote Philippians 1:6: "He who began a good work in you will carry it on to completion until the day of Christ Jesus"? Or the overused "All things work together for good to those who love God" (Romans 8:28, NKJV)? Frequently, we are reminded of God's love in the midst of trials, as in the words of the song "Sometimes He Calms the Storm," sung by Christian recording artist Scott Krippayne.

> Sometimes He calms the storm
> With a whispered "peace be still"
> He can settle any sea

But it doesn't mean He will

Sometimes He holds us close
And lets the wind and waves go wild
Sometimes He calms the storm
And other times He calms His child[1]

The Bible identifies the remedy for joblessness by giving us the opportunity to work in God's harvest field. Matthew 20:6, 7 reads,

> "He asked them, 'Why have you been standing here all day long doing nothing?'
>   " 'Because no one has hired us,' they answered.
> "He said to them, 'You also go and work in my vineyard.' "

Automatically, I hear the words, *You're hired.* I do not know about you, but these are reassuring words to me. *You're hired!* Have you ever heard them? I have.

What is our purpose here on earth? I believe that we are already at earth's eleventh hour, just like in Jesus' parable. Let's review the story in verses 1–7 of Matthew 20:

> "For the kingdom of heaven is like a landowner who went out early in the morning to hire workers for his vineyard. He agreed to pay them a denarius for the day and sent them into his vineyard.
> "About nine in the morning he went out and saw others standing in the marketplace doing nothing. He told them, 'You also go and work in my vineyard, and I will pay you whatever is right.' So they went.
> "He went out again about noon and about three in the afternoon and did the same thing. About five in the afternoon he went out and found still others standing around. He asked them, 'Why have you been standing here all day long doing nothing?'
>   " 'Because no one has hired us,' they answered.
> "He said to them, 'You also go and work in my vineyard.' "

In other words, *you're hired.*

What do you do when you're hired by God? God says, "All the days ordained for me were written in your book before one of them came to be" (Psalm 139:16).

God knows each day's plan, but sometimes we feel like we are in between His purposes. Daily I was praying for God to do something for my brother Mark. Meanwhile Corleen and I were preparing for the CLASSeminar.

Turning passion into action

The preparation paid off, because the day before the CLASSeminar we had 110 people signed up. The seminar is designed to equip women and men to turn their God-given passions for speaking and writing into ministries or enhance the ministries they already have. The purpose is to turn passion into action. Learning how experts speak and write is a great way to sharpen your testimony to work in the vineyard. CLASSeminar uses the insightful text of 2 Timothy 2:2 as its theme: "The things [the doctrine, the precepts, the admonitions, the sum of my ministry] which you have heard me teach in the presence of many witnesses, entrust [as a treasure] to reliable and faithful men who will also be capable and qualified to teach others" (AMP).

On the Sunday before the CLASSeminar was to start, we had several people dashing about running errands. Corleen stayed at the venue to do some last-minute decorating. "May I pick up Florence Littauer at the airport?" my husband asked me many months before April 7, 2002. Ron had been anxiously waiting to meet Florence. He got to know her through her tapes, which we listened to in the car on long drives. Today was the day, and he sped off to the airport.

Remember my prayer from the September 2000 CLASSeminar? It felt like God was saying to pray that my small-group instructor Georgia would be my friend. So I prayed, "Lord, I like Georgia. I know this sounds improbable, but You can do anything. I would like to see her again. Maybe become friends. Would You arrange that?" Well, God remembers everything, and I thought it was very interesting that God brought Georgia Shaffer to the West Coast of the United States for this event. I was delighted to pick up Georgia and her friend Marita Littauer at the airport myself. "Hello, Marita and Georgia. Georgia, do you remember me from the Orlando CLASSeminar?" I asked.

"Yes, yes, I think I do remember you," she replied.

Eleven CLASSeminar staff members and about nine Women's Ministries Department helpers and some spouses enjoyed a wonderful potluck meal before Florence was to speak on Sunday night. This gave us a great opportunity to mingle with the CLASSeminar staff. Georgia wanted to meet my husband. Ron and Georgia soon began talking about the United States Civil War. "Oh, you live near Gettysburg?" he asked. "I love Civil War history. I have been studying it since grade school. Diane and I would love to see more of the East Coast. We've only been there once."

"When you make plans next time, why don't you stay at my house?" Georgia said.

"Thank you; that would be nice," he answered. I thought to myself, *What are the odds of that happening?* On Sunday night, more than four hundred people packed the church to hear Florence give a special presentation. This resulted in fifteen more people signing up to make our attendance 125— one of the highest-attended CLASSeminars.

After attending the CLASSeminar, Laurie Berning said, "My family benefited from my new knowledge of the personalities. They wanted to hear all about them. It is so important knowing who you are and how to effectively communicate."

Myrna Giesbrecht, who referred to herself as "the smile in the front row," said, "The show-not-tell method of instruction Marita and Florence modeled is so valuable in transferring information. CLASSeminar was so incredibly uplifting and invigorating. I came away supercharged and confirmed in what I had heard God calling me to do. It took me ten hours to drive home instead of eight. Several times I had to pull over and take notes."

God working on the job request

The odds of something happening are great when we respond to God's prompting. Ron and I could not get the conversation with Georgia out of our minds, so in September 2002, we traveled to Pennsylvania to tour Gettysburg and other Civil War sites and stayed with Georgia. Ron is passionate about using his video camera and has captured many of our trips for scenic showings later. While stepping up to a curb on the way to a museum, Ron's camera fell out of his hand and hit the ground. "It felt like someone pushed it out of my hand," he said, as if questioning why and how it happened.

The next morning Ron and I toured some Amish towns, then came back to eat at Georgia's house. Georgia and I were able to discuss and pray about some decisions she needed to make. The next morning, as I was reading my Bible, I felt impressed to share with her two scriptures in Acts. One was Acts 20:22: "And now, compelled by the Spirit, I am going to Jerusalem, not knowing what will happen to me there." I especially put emphasis on the first part, "And now, compelled by the Spirit." Really, looking back, it is easy to see how God compels us to go different places and share various things with people. Yet, as I left Georgia's house, I could not help but wonder what would happen now to my prayer request to be friends.

When Ron and I arrived home, I asked, "What are you going to do with the video camera?" He replied, "It would cost too much to fix the video part, but it can take good still pictures. Maybe I will give it to a friend of mine."

"Can we give it to my brother?" I was compelled to say.

"Mark," I called him immediately, "can you come over to our house? We have something we want to give you." I provided no additional information till he arrived.

"Ron dropped this on our vacation, and it won't take video pictures anymore, but it will take still pictures. Can you use this for a camera?" I asked. His face brightened, "I was just thinking about becoming a realtor; but there are so many costs involved, and one of them would be a camera for taking pictures of houses. I think this is a sign I should be a realtor." Today Mark is a successful realtor and is happily married to a woman named Heather. Amazing! Looking back, it is easy to see the God moments when He allows us to be a link in a chain, so to speak, for others. I do not want to miss them in the future.

God is involved in every little detail for working in His vineyard. Are you out of work? You are hired in God's vineyard.

Moments of Reflection:

1. Do you have a job? Do you think of it as separate from your "job" for the Lord? Compare and contrast.

2. Journal or share with others about a time when Jesus was involved in your life.

---

1. Benton Kevin Stokes and Tony W. Wood, songwriters, "Sometimes He Calms the Storm," MetroLyrics, accessed November 30, 2015, http://www.metrolyrics.com/sometimes-he-calms-the-storm-lyrics-scott-krippayne.html. "Sometimes He Calms the Storm" copyright © Universal Music Publishing Group.

CHAPTER SIXTEEN

Every Life Makes a Difference

For You created my inmost being;
you knit me together in my mother's womb. . . .
All the days ordained for me were written in your book
before one of them came to be.
—*Psalm 139:13, 16*

O ne day at the office, a man from another department rounded the corner and sat down to talk with me. "I received a difficult call from a mother whose daughter is not speaking to her," he said, looking pensive. He then added, "Her daughter is going to have an abortion, and she asked me to call her daughter for her and talk her out of it. I don't think this person's daughter is going to listen to a man, and I see Corleen is out today. The daughter is having her abortion soon. Will you call her? I'll understand if you feel uncomfortable and don't want to."

"I'll pray about it and call her," I responded while thinking, *But I'm not a mother. What could I say?*

"Here's her number," he said, then stood to leave. Bowing my head in prayer and beginning to wonder about the gravity of the situation, I started praying. Soon my mind was absorbed by a life-changing story I could share.

Life-changing twist

In the 1960s, there was a couple who were unable to have children. The childless couple had prayed for four years, to no avail. One day a doctor they knew phoned to say, "I am delivering a baby soon for a young couple who do not wish to keep their child. Do you want it?" In that era, a woman who did not want her child frequently gave up the baby for adoption.

Surprised and thrilled by the good news, they responded, "Yes!"

When the child was born, the potential parents started packing to go visit the child but were interrupted by a phone call from the hospital. "We regret to inform you that all plans have been halted because a heart murmur has been detected. You won't be able to afford a needed surgery, and this child should be put in an institution, so the state can deal with the expense of a heart surgery."

"What? But this is the child we have been praying for," said the father as he held the phone.

"We are awarding the child to a 'friend of the baby' represented by the state, and you can talk to that person," said the hospital staff member. Crestfallen, the potential parents knelt on the floor to pray. People in the couple's church told them, "You don't want a defective child; wait for another one." But they felt this was the child God planned for them to have and desperately clung to the idea. Seventeen long days later they were told, "You can come and look at the baby through the hospital window before she goes into foster care." More weeks of waiting, and they took another trip to be questioned by the "friend of the baby." Meanwhile a court date was set to have a hearing to decide if the parents could adopt this child who would need a surgery.

"She's so beautiful. She is the best-looking baby I have ever seen," said the father as they looked through the window. Five more weeks went by till the court appearance. Finally, the day arrived. The judge asked a few questions and decided to give them their little girl. A side door opened, and the "friend of the baby" walked in with *me*; on that day, my new parents went home with *me* in their arms.

Nine years later and shortly before my heart surgery, I made a renewed commitment to the Lord. My parents were both sitting beside my bed. My father spoke, "The doctor said we didn't need to tell you. But we need you to know there is a chance you might not survive the surgery. We know we will see you in heaven later, but right now do you want to recommit your life to the Lord?"

Without hesitation, I responded, "Yes, I love Jesus, and commit my life to Him."

My parents had been upfront with me my whole life about being adopted and that a heart surgery would have to take place when my heart grew large enough. Every six months we went to a cardiologist to take EKG pictures and have a consultation. My parents often shared that God gave me to them and God was in charge of my life, so from an early age, I had faith that God had a purpose for me.

Fearfully and wonderfully made

Have you ever faced a surgery and thought, *What happens if I don't make it through?* Sometimes we have warning in advance; other times we do not get prior warning. When we surrender our lives to Jesus or rededicate our lives to Him, we have peace during the unknown. What a difference one life can make. As we put our lives in the Lord's hands, we become tools for huge eternal results. Psalm 139:13–16 shares,

> For you created my inmost being;
>> you knit me together in my mother's womb.
> I praise you because I am fearfully and wonderfully made;
>> your works are wonderful,
>> I know that full well.
> My frame was not hidden from you
>> when I was made in the secret place,
>> when I was woven together in the depths of the earth.
> Your eyes saw my unformed body;
>> all the days ordained for me were written in your book
>> before one of them came to be.

Now as I thought about how my life turned out, I wanted to encourage another person that God could make a difference in hers also. One life and one decision can make a difference. I placed the call to the daughter who was about to have an abortion and reached an answering machine. "God through me" left a heartfelt message and prayed. Since I knew God can accomplish much through prayer, I felt at peace. The Bible says intercession for others is important and necessary. First Timothy 2:1 shares, "I urge, then, first of all, that petitions, prayers, intercession and thanksgiving be made for all people." T. W. Hunt, a Southern Baptist prayer leader, is credited with making this assertion, "Of biblical prayers that we know have been answered, 78 percent involve intercession."[1]

I praise the Lord I grew up with a Christian family that shared Jesus and prayed in faith for needs we were experiencing. Sometimes we had to wait. Sometimes God gave a special blessing soon in order to build our faith. As a result, I always felt a close relationship to the Lord.

Wilderness experience

During my wilderness experience with no job in 1999, I read Stormie

Omartian's book *Just Enough Light for the Step I'm On*. Stormie said, "If you are at a place in your life where you feel like you can't take one step without the Lord's help, be glad. He has you where He wants you. . . . God has you on this path, no matter how difficult and impossible it may seem right now, because you are willing to follow Him. *He* wants to accomplish great things *through you* that can only come out of a life of faith. He wants your undivided attention because you can't do these things on your own."[2]

I would not have it any other way. I want to be one of those "crazy" prayer people that make a difference for God. Remember our first job is Acts 20:24—testifying to the gospel of God's grace. It is not a "go-to" job when all else fails; it is our job.

In April 2014, I shared with the Lord, "I would like to go to Bellingham and say a prayer of thanksgiving for awarding me to my parents fifty years ago. Do You like the idea? We could go to the courthouse and tour some museums to get the flavor of the times back then." When God opened up the opportunity to preach in the Bellingham, Washington, Seventh-day Adventist Church in July, Ron and I made the trek to Bellingham. This was one month after the anniversary date when my parents were awarded custody of me. I had not been to the Bellingham courthouse since. As I sat on the courthouse steps and tried to imagine my parents walking up those stairs many years ago, I was flooded with gratefulness for all God had accomplished. God and I shared some moments of thanks together. The next day, Sabbath, after the sermon, I noticed a group of people praying in the pew. When they came to the lobby, one shared, "It is an interesting idea you have about on-site praying, and we are going to try it."

Prayers in places of significance

Have you ever traveled to a place of significance and had a thank-you prayer in the actual spot your memorable event occurred? Jacob in Genesis 28 had a memorable God-intervention moment. Jacob had tricked his father into believing he was his older brother, Esau, so his father had given him the birthright blessing. When Esau heard, he was furious and vowed to kill Jacob. Assuming the worst, Jacob fled for his life. The first night of his journey he had a dream of a stairway from heaven to the earth with angels ascending and descending on it. Before continuing on his journey, he named the place Bethel; verse 16 describes, "When Jacob awoke from his sleep, he thought, 'Surely the LORD is in this place, and I was not aware of it.' " More than twenty years later, God called him back to Bethel for worship and dedication. So many emotions swept over Jacob as he remembered all God had done for him since that day when his life seemed so uncertain.

Sensing that his family needed to set all other gods aside, Jacob told them to destroy their idols, wash themselves, and put on clean clothing (Genesis 35:2). God loves it when we return to Him with all our hearts, and He did something special for Jacob by appearing and sharing words of confirmation. Verses 9, 10 share, "God appeared to [Jacob] again at Bethel. God blessed him, saying, 'Your name is Jacob, but you will not be called Jacob any longer. From now on your name will be Israel.' So God renamed him Israel" (NLT). Verses 14, 15 state, "Jacob set up a stone pillar to mark the place where God had spoken to him. Then he poured wine over it as an offering to God and anointed the pillar with olive oil. And Jacob named the place Bethel (which means 'house of God'), because God had spoken to him there."

In the same way, God calls us to return. Sometimes it is a call to give thanks (such as the one leper who was cleansed), or it is a call to return to the place where we first made a commitment, or a it is a place of rest in His promises that "God, who began the good work within you, will continue his work until it is finally finished on the day when Christ Jesus returns" (Philippians 1:6, NLT). Always Jesus is calling. His life makes a difference for us, and His life through us makes a difference.

Moments of Reflection:

1. Are you in the middle of making a decision that you are unsure about? Call out to Jesus for help, then call or visit someone who can compassionately listen and pray for your decision.

2. Have you ever taken a moment or a vacation to renew your commitment to Jesus?

3. Take a moment right now to pray this dedication prayer, "Lord Jesus, I rededicate myself to You. Please forgive me of any sins or idols I might be attracted to. Please take them from me because I may not have the strength to give them to You. Thank You for shedding Your blood on the cross and standing in my place so that I can have eternal life. Thank You for Your Holy Spirit that guides my life. Take my life and be a blessing to others through me. Amen."

---

1. "Evangelism–GPS," Baptist Convention of Maryland/Delaware, accessed June 17, 2014, http://bcmd.org/evangelism-gps/.

2. Stormie Omartian, *Just Enough Light for the Step I'm On* (Eugene, OR: Harvest House Publishers, 1999), 15; emphasis added.

CHAPTER SEVENTEEN

Stuck for a Reason

"For I, the LORD your God, will hold your right hand,
saying to you, 'Fear not, I will help you.' "
—Isaiah 41:13, NKJV

I loathe the helpless feeling of being stuck. Whether it is thick-falling snow hiding the road ahead; a cold so penetrating, no amount of layering stops the shuddering; or vehicles stopped for miles because conditions cause careening cars to collide. Sometimes I can feel in advance that something is not right. One time, when I was small, my family vacationed at the beach, and the day we were to come back I was full of dread. "We need to stay at the beach and not leave today. We need to stay here. Let's not go today," I urged.

"We have to leave today. Dad has to work tomorrow," my mother replied with logic. Several miles into our journey I tried again. "We need to turn around and go back." Ever notice no one else can hear the Holy Spirit prompting you in your own head? And sometimes parents discount this in children. Or maybe that was my perspective. Then again, sometimes we discount it ourselves.

That day my family came back from the beach, and about an hour into our journey, my mother heard a distinct voice in her head, *Put on your seat belt; put on your seat belt!* The Holy Spirit was prompting my mother. My mother looked for her seat belt, but it was tucked under the back of the seat. She tried to dig it out but then gave up. The Holy Spirit impressed again, *Put on your seat belt; put on your seat belt!* Providentially, my mother responded and tried again to find the seat belt, dug it out, and fastened it. One mile later my father was driving at highway speeds as a car pulled out directly in front of us. Our car was instantly crushed. It was traumatic for a ten-year-old to watch as my mother was put on a stretcher and hauled away.

Soon a policeman interrupted my thoughts. "Would you like to sit in my warm police car?" My brother and I stood helplessly by the crumpled accordion, formerly the front end of our car, steam still coming out of the hood. However, I did not want to do anything but be with my mother.

"Dear Jesus, please save my mother," I prayed silently.

"It's all right; I need to talk with these people. You can go with the policeman," my father confirmed to us while dabbing blood from his face.

"Can you take me to my mother?" I asked the policeman pleadingly.

"I'm sorry, honey, it's going to be a while. The hospital will take care of her. Let's go over to my car." My younger brother and I climbed in. Mark kept asking me questions while I was praying in my head. We were stuck! Stuck not knowing what was happening to our mother. Stuck waiting for someone to take us to the hospital. I hate being stuck in the unknown.

"She's going to fall; catch . . ." my mother started to say weakly, but no one heard. We had finally made it to the hospital. I took one look at my mother, fainted backward, and hit my head so hard that the nurses put me in a bed across from my mother. My mother had large bruises for close to a year. And it was years later that she revisited the accident story and shared how the Holy Spirit had prompted her twice about the seat belt. Choked with feelings, no amount of words can ever express my gratitude that she listened and responded.

At times, we ignore the inner motivations of the Holy Spirit. One day I was at my parent's house, sitting in the dining room reading the newspaper. "Go into the bathroom to stand by your mother," I could sense the Holy Spirit prompting. *No,* I thought, *She is doing the same thing she always does when she helps my father.* Moments later I heard screaming and a thud as my father with late-stage Alzheimer's fell backward.

Oh no! I had advance warning. I could have steadied him, I thought. Why, at times, do we not react to the Holy Spirit?

Duly warned!

The 2003 women's retreat in Sunriver, Oregon, began with good weather, but winter weather changes rapidly. On Saturday night, snow fell, and we awoke Sunday morning to some icy spots, but many ladies were very excited about it—some even relating this was an answer to prayer. As I entered into the Homestead lobby where the main meeting would soon begin, I noticed out of the corner of my eye a woman fast approaching me from my left. Sticking out her hand, she said, "Hi, I'm Bev Schultz. You probably won't remember my name because you meet so many people. However, I just wanted to tell you, you did a great job with your talk. But I can't wait to hear you in ten years, you'll be even better." In my head, my mind was saying, "Bev Schultz, Bev Schultz, Bev Schultz" over and over so I would not forget her name. Also, I could not help but wonder about the ten years she talked about. Despite that I said, "Thanks; nice to meet you. Ten years is a long time. I'll be, oh, I guess I'll still be young." Bev continued, "I live in Madras, which you will pass through on your way home." Bev told me other details about Madras, Oregon. One of my parting comments was, "Well, the weather isn't looking very good for our travel home."

The Holy Spirit was probably speaking through Bev as she countered, "I travel all the time in snow, you'll be fine. Just don't delay too long before leaving."

"Well, that is partly up to Corleen since we are riding together," I said as we walked toward the meeting.

Delayed!

"A lady named Carol* fell on the ice and hit her head. Her friends have taken her to the hospital in Bend," Corleen looked sad as she met me in the hallway with these words. After the meeting, Corleen and I hurried to pack. We were the last ones to leave the event, and I urged, "This wetness is going to turn to ice after a few hours; we could stay here and wait till tomorrow."

Corleen replied, "We have everything all packed, and we are already in motion, so let's keep going. If Carol is still in the hospital, I want to see her." Hunger overtook us, and we stopped at Taco Bell on the way. When we reached the hospital, we discovered Carol was no longer there.

"Corleen, I think we are delayed too much now to keep going. It's going to get icy, and we won't make it all the way home. We need to stop somewhere."

"No, we will make it. Let's keep going," Corleen replied.

Two are better than one

I have learned in my years of working with a different personality that also prays hard and listens to the Holy Spirit that my input and Corleen's input, together, seem to always put us in the right spot, at the right time for God's purposes. Even if what we were experiencing at the moment was not pleasant, it was useful for God's bigger picture. I tried to keep quiet and pray silently as we continued down the road with nightfall an hour away and more than two hours of driving left—if conditions were good. But they

---

* Carol is a pseudonym.

were not. Just past Redmond, as we approached a curved overpass, we halted because traffic was stopped in the middle. A jackknifed semitrailer took up the whole road, and cars were just inching past on the shoulder. In addition, cars were sliding in every direction. A smaller truck tried to go around us, slipped and stopped, causing any progress to cease. We were now stuck. We waited an hour, still stuck.

Looking out into the blackness, I started to think about a bathroom. "Oh no, I need to go to the bathroom," looking this way and that way, taking it all in—no tall trees, only clear landscape and one small house six hundred yards away.

"Oh, God, You have to help me," I started saying this over and over. "You have to get me out of this situation. I can't stay here all night!" I did not include Corleen in the prayer because she looked so calm and did not seem to need to go to the bathroom. Shortly, Corleen said, "I'm praying for you, Diane. You're going to make it. You could get out of the van and walk the six hundred yards to a tree or go to that house."

"No," I lamented, "the minute I get out of the van, traffic will move. You'll have to move forward, and there's no place to pull over." Waves like the ocean, first of calm and then of lament washed over me, one after the other. I let negative thoughts crowd in. *Why did we stop in Bend? If we hadn't stopped in Bend, we would be an hour farther down the road. We should have left Sunriver sooner. We should have taken that little road we just passed; maybe it went around.*

Just then, like a logjam breaking up, cars started moving slightly, one by one, and we were around.

"Oh, *finally*. Thank You, Lord," I sighed heavily. Then I started up again, "This is awful; we shouldn't have to drive in this ice the whole way home. It's dark. There will be more problems, and it will take way too long. We need to stop in Madras," I lamented to Corleen. She appeared to be thinking.

"Do you still need to go to the bathroom?" she questioned.

"No, I can wait till Madras. Let's keep going," I responded.

"What? After all that?" she replied.

"I can wait," I said, my mind now focused on our new destination. Twenty-five minutes later and a couple of stoplights into Madras, one light turned red, and Corleen tapped the brakes and slid through the intersection.

"You're right," she said. "We should stop."

Instantly sizing up the situation, I replied, "There's a motel down there on the left."

"It's a good thing you stopped, they have been turning people around up ahead. A horse trailer is jackknifed in the road going out of Warm Springs. Yeah, it's real bad out there," the hotel clerk said as we walked into the lobby. She continued, "My husband is feeding food to a homeless boy right now in the back." My ears perked up. Could this be why we were here in Madras? God wants prayer for a homeless boy? I started to pray silently. Out loud I said, "I guess he could use some extra prayer too."

"Yes, he could," she responded. Now I was getting excited as a purpose began to form in my mind. Inside our hotel room as I unpacked, words suddenly came out of my lips, "If I'm going to be stuck in this town, then I'm going to pray for this town! Corleen, let's go prayer walk the whole town! We can go up one side and down the other." She agreed, and we set off in the black night and icy sidewalks. We prayed for a Laundromat, a school, a park, the cars and trucks that passed, the businesses—everything we saw as we went up the one way road and down the other side—and finally walked into an Assembly of God church that looked open. We sat in on their Sunday evening service, and when the pastor closed his sermon, he invited people to come up for prayer. Everyone stood, so Corleen put on her coat. "Let's go up front to pray for the pastor instead of him praying for us," I beckoned. She agreed, and we shared a nice time with the pastor. By midday the next day, the ice melted, and we were on our way.

Stuck again in Madras

One month later Lee Haynes, the scheduler for churches that needed a speaker, said, "Say, you ought to preach in Madras."

"When do you need someone?" I asked.

"January 10, 2004," she replied.

"Watch," I said, "I'll get stuck in the ice again." As if foreshadowing this, the entire city of Portland was covered in ice and snow the whole week before. "Lord, please open a window of opportunity," I prayed all week. On Friday, January 9, I drove over Mount Hood to Madras with ice on both sides and in the middle of the road. The road was only clear in the grooves made by the cars before me. Upon reaching the hotel, ice pellets started to fall. I took my bags to my room and called Corleen. "It feels like I'm going to be stuck here again, so Sabbath I want to leave right after church to arrive back before dark," I lamented. We prayed, and the morning dawned with a blue sky and was beautiful. What a relief as I peered through the drapes, but the streets remained icy. I grabbed my Bible, and it fell open to Isaiah 52:12:

But you will not leave in haste
　　or go in flight;
for the LORD will go before you,
　　the God of Israel will be your rear guard.

I sighed, "What now?"

Still intending to leave right after church, after the sermon, I made my way to the lobby to greet people. Bev, from the earlier retreat, drew close and asked, "Can you come over for lunch?"

I responded, "How far away do you live?"

Bev replied, "Two miles up on a hill. You can ride with us because our hill is all iced over."

"I have four-wheel drive and can make it. I will follow you," I reassured her, still wanting to leave as soon as I could. However, as soon as I sat down at their dining table and looked at the gorgeous view of Mount Jefferson that filled the window, I changed my mind. I melted into a serene calm as it dawned on me. *The Lord has put me in the right spot. I love this view.* It was with great hesitation that I left later and grasped Bev's hand in thanks. God spoke to me, *"Pray that she will be your friend."*

It's easy to look back and see answers to your prayers. Looking forward, we pray by faith that yes, God *loves* to be involved in our lives. Luke 18:1 says, "Then Jesus told his disciples a parable to show them that they should always pray and not give up." Dennis Smith, in his book *40 Days,* comments on this passage, "The purpose of this parable was to teach us the necessity of persevering in prayer. Luke knew Jesus taught that we ought, or should (NIV), always pray and not faint, or stop praying, until we get the answer. The Greek form of the verb pray is continuous action."[1]

Months later I called Bev when I knew I was traveling through Madras. My friend Cheryl and I met Bev for hiking and lunch. While looking over the menu, I glanced up and saw Bev pull out a clear retainer from her teeth. "What's that?" I asked.

"It's called Invisalign, for straightening my teeth, and we can straighten yours too," she asserted. (Bev's husband, Wayne, is a dentist.)

What a bold statement to make. No one has ever told me I have crooked teeth, I thought. I said, "Well, I have pondered this before, and, sure, you can have Wayne take a look." My new choleric friend picked up her cell phone and had Wayne meet us at the office.

From Madras to mission

Thus began my journey over the mountain to Madras for dental work every eight weeks for more than two years. And, yes, most times I stayed at Bev and Wayne's house. Twice, snow and ice made me turn around to stay another night. *What is up with this town? It really needs prayer!* I thought, dialing Corleen to request prayer each time.

On February 11, 2007, God gave me another opportunity to preach in Madras. It was during that day that I had the thought. *You know this would be a good town for a mission trip.* Picking up the phone, "Corleen, I feel compelled that . . ."

Corleen and I started praying about a mission trip to Madras and formed a team with Bev Schultz and Pastor Frank and April McNeil of the Madras Seventh-day Adventist Church. To make a long story short, in June 2008, fifty volunteers and thirty-three members of the Madras church accomplished a huge undertaking for a week of outreach we called Hope in the Park. We helped with several community projects: building a Habitat for Humanity home, remodeling the Madras Gospel Mission, painting the county food bank, landscaping and weeding, and more. Each evening townspeople came to the park for a Vacation Bible School, booths of various types, a drama presentation, concerts by community and professional musicians, and a speaker delivering hope-filled messages. The DeCoster's Kids Anti-Drug, Anti-Violence Suzuki Dream Team, with its sixty-foot-long trailer, went to different locations in town each day with anti-drug and anti-alcohol displays and, yes, motorcycles. Each kid who signed the anti-drug pledge received a free subscription to *Winner* magazine.

On Saturday night, when a thunderstorm forced us to move our evening program to the church, Corleen protested, "But, Lord, we will lose them. They won't move to the church. They will just go home." But God proved her wrong! The church was full and overflowing into the lobby. Afterward one visitor commented, "I have never experienced such a wonderful worship service!"

Have you ever been stuck? It might have been for a reason. It is amazing to look back and see how God can intervene in our moments of crisis and bring glory to Himself.

Moments of Reflection:

1. Make a list of important unanswered plans that you feel Jesus is still working on, and claim promises with your group or journal your prayers for these items.

2. Share a moment when God intervened because you were stuck. If you feel God is still working on the details, then praise Him for what will happen in the future. "Now faith is confidence in what we hope for and assurance about what we do not see" (Hebrews 11:1).

---

1. Dennis Smith, *40 Days* (Hagerstown, MD: Review and Herald® Publishing Association, 2010), 52.

CHAPTER EIGHTEEN

Angel Involvement

Suddenly a great company of the heavenly host appeared with the angel,
praising God and saying, "Glory to God in the highest heaven,
and on earth peace to those on whom his favor rests."
—Luke 2:13, 14

A local church has a walkthrough Christmas Nativity event every year, and I signed up to be a flying angel. Hanging fifteen feet above the ground, I was to exclaim, "Glory to God in the highest heaven, and on earth peace" (Luke 2:14). Corleen and I planned to take turns as the flying angel. We were to be connected to a motor-driven cable that carried us out of a shed while hovering over a scene of shepherds, sheep, and community people, to make a heavenly proclamation. About an hour before the event was to begin, I walked up to the scene and saw Corleen hanging on the cable while men feverishly worked on the motor. She was stuck in midair. They could not get her to go forward or backward. I looked up at her and said, "This was my worry that I would be the one who would get stuck. And now you are stuck."

A few men fixed the motor shortly after people started going through the first scene. (We were the fourth scene.) Since Corleen was already strapped in, she made the angelic proclamation for the first couple of hours and all went smoothly. Then it was my turn to be the angel. The "platform" we stood on was a large five-gallon paint bucket. When I was clipped to the line, I soon realized there was no way to get comfortable. My harness pulled up and pressed into me while I stood. *Corleen didn't seem to have pain, so why does this feel uncomfortable?* I thought. Both of my feet had to remain in one spot, or the bucket would tip over. As time wore on, I became increasingly uncomfortable. *If the machine breaks down again, I will be left hanging while they try to fix it.* I tried not to think about this. Corleen flipped the switch, and the cable carried me out to hover over the scene. It was then that I realized the harness pressed into my neck and ribs, causing me to take shallow breaths. When the motor brought me back, I began grumbling to Corleen. After several more trips out, I began to dread the shallower breathing and the pain this harness caused me. What happened next was absolutely unexpected.

On one trip out to share the angel's proclamation, I beheld at least thirty angels lighting up the sky behind the shepherds! They hung in space like it was normal to be there. Incredible! God sent real angels to encourage me. I was amazed and impressed by the sight, then I wondered, *Did they show up just because I was discouraged and in pain, or was it to show they cared about our drama depicting Christ's birth?*

Angels from heaven

"Suddenly a great company of the heavenly host appeared with the angel, praising God and saying, 'Glory to God in the highest' " (verse 13). *Were these some of the angels that came to make the original proclamation?* I wondered. Their presence was palpable and calming. I felt repentant of my grumbling. They stayed while our human angel choir sang after my proclamation. I was speechless and grateful to have witnessed such a sight. Standing on my paint bucket moments later, I looked at Corleen and did not know what to say.

"I'm sorry I keep grumbling," I finally managed. "I just saw real angels!"

There were several more trips out to make the angelic proclamation to groups of people witnessing our scene. The pain from the harness did not let up, and I had a hard time holding back a grumble or two. Then my worst fear was realized—the motor gave out while I was still ten feet from my landing spot. *Uh-oh, what now?* I thought while taking in shallow breaths. A helper named Frank ran up to stand under me, so I could teeter on his shoulders. *Whew, that is better!* I took in a few deeper breaths. Corleen was flipping the switch up and down, trying to get the motor to work. *Creeeeaak!* The motor suddenly plunged me five feet backward. My feet just barely touched a flat surface behind me a few feet from the paint bucket. I managed to grab the sides of the wooden doorway, but this was worse because I was pitched forward and now could not breathe. I thought I was in pain before, but this felt much worse. "Corleen, make them get me down! Corleen, make them get me down," I told my friend.

She responded, "I'm praying."

I replied, "It's not helping!" Just then Frank ran for a ladder and propped it up on the side of the shed, so I could step on to it. It was at an awkward angle, because I was still connected to the main line, and my arm muscles began to ache in addition to the other issues.

More flips of the switch, and I flew backward off the ladder past the paint bucket and hit the back of the shed before coming forward to land on the paint bucket. I gasped in and out for breath and shook my head in disbelief that my worst fear had just happened.

Corleen asked, "Do you want me to finish out the night for you?"

Then I remembered the angels. "No, I'll keep going," I responded.

He is Christ the Lord

At home the next morning, I shuddered at the thought of two more nights of potential agony and went downstairs to complain to the Lord about my predicament and to ask for help.

"Lord, I can't move more than a few inches on that paint bucket, and the harness is cinched up around me. There is no relief the whole time. I can't breathe right, and it is uncomfortable," I muttered. Instantly, the Lord gave me the thought of Jesus on the cross, unable to move, arms held in place. I paused to imagine it: He had to push up on His feet, held by a nail, to take a breath.

His breathing grew labored.

No one said, "I'm praying for You."

No one offered Him a ladder.

No one flipped a switch up and down to get Him unstuck.

No one was working on the motor.

No one tried to get Him down.

Instead people ridiculed Him and told Him to take Himself down. " 'You who are going to destroy the temple and build it in three days, save yourself! Come down from the cross, if you are the Son of God!' . . . 'He saved others,' they said, 'but he can't save himself! . . . Let him come down now from the cross, and we will believe in him' " (Matthew 27:40, 42).

Blood came out of His head. Jesus was not wearing five layers of clothing (like I was) to protect Himself.

As I paused to imagine the scene that God impressed me with, I was awestruck. However, my choleric, logical nature took over, and I said, "But this is not a comparison to me. I am not dying on a cross to save people."

The Lord replied immediately, *But you are saving people!* So I had to persevere. I had to go on sharing my testimony in the drama, "Glory to God in the highest, and peace on earth!" I proclaimed (Luke 2:14, author's adaptation). "Do not be afraid. I bring you good news of great joy for all people. Today in Bethlehem, the city of David, a Savior has been born to you. He is Christ the Lord. This will be a sign to you, you will find a baby wrapped in cloths and lying in a manger" (verses 11, 12, author's adaptation).

I feel honored by the Lord for letting me see behind the scenes. I feel honored to be saving people through seemingly ordinary tasks and overjoyed that God sometimes presses close when we feel discouraged and helpless.

Moments of Reflection:

1. Take a moment to share scripture promises about persevering in prayer with your group.

2. What is the testimony God is asking you to share?

3. Jesus' love for us held Him in place on the cross, and our names are written in His heart. Take a moment to thank Him.

CHAPTER NINETEEN

Opportunities and Connections

Peter saw his opportunity and addressed the crowd.
—*Acts 3:12, NLT*

God uses all kinds of methods to get our attention when His people need our prayers and help. On September 18, 2003, I was flying back from Spokane after visiting friends. As I stood in the Southwest A line to get on the plane, I counted six men in front of me. As I assumed this meant I would not be sitting on the front row, I knew that the left side would have a better view of Mount Hood when I got close to Portland. However, when I boarded the plane, I suddenly felt compelled to sit on the right side, veered right, and sat down. *Now why did I do that?* I thought. *I won't have the best view. I could still move over there. No, I don't feel like it.*

Soon a woman in her midtwenties asked, "May I sit in the middle, next to you?"

"Sure," I responded.

We started conversing in the usual airplane banter.

"Why are you going to Portland?" she asked.

"I live there," I said.

"What do you do there?" she asked.

"I work in a women's ministries department at the conference level. We provide resources for more than one hundred churches."

"That's interesting, I have a friend that works in women's ministries. Do you know ——?" She shared a name I did not know. "I'm a Seventh-day Adventist, so maybe that is why I don't know her," I answered. She was heading to Portland because her boyfriend lived there, and she wanted to relocate.

The plane suddenly bounced.

"Was that turbulence?" she asked.

I thought to myself, *If she thinks this is turbulence, she doesn't ride planes much.*

I responded, "Well, I suppose you could call that a little turbulence. Now if you really want to hear about turbulence, you should have been on our flight to the Philippines. Our women's ministries group went there on an evangelistic trip. The plane was shaking up and down violently, and people were clinging to their rosary beads and praying fervently." Then I thought, *You know, I bet she is Catholic, and I shouldn't have said that.*

She answered, "My mother goes on mission trips to Guatemala with her church and builds houses." She added, "I was raised Catholic, but I'm looking for a different church. And maybe the Seventh-day Adventist Church is the right one; I don't know. My mother tells me I need to go to a priest and confess my sins, but I think I can go directly to God."

"Yes, I believe you are right that we can go directly to Jesus. I've been to the Vatican, you know." I told her briefly about how St. Peter's Basilica was built because a man named Tetzel raised money selling indulgences for people's sins during Martin Luther's time. And that God steadily brought His people out of the Dark Ages by revealing truths, such as grace, through Luther, the Holy Spirit as the Bible's only interpreter through Ulrich Zwingli, and calling us to holy living by John Wesley.

"I didn't know those ideas came from so long ago," she said.

After that, there was a lull in the conversation.

When we were almost to Portland, I asked, "May I pray with you about finding the right church?"

"Yes, please do," she responded. So I prayed.

Biblical sharing

Just like Peter and John on their way to the temple in Acts 3, you never know what a day will bring. Acts 3:1–6 shares,

> One day Peter and John were going up to the temple at the time of prayer—at three in the afternoon. Now a man who was lame from birth was being carried to the temple gate called Beautiful, where he was put every day to beg from those going into the temple courts. When he saw Peter and John about to enter, he asked them for money. Peter looked straight at him, as did John. Then Peter said, "Look at us!" So the man gave them his attention, expecting to get something from them.
>
> Then Peter said, "Silver or gold I do not have, but what I do have I give you. In the name of Jesus Christ of Nazareth, walk."

You could call it a divine intervention set up by God to have them in the right place at the right time to change a life. The Jews observed three times of prayer: 9 A.M., 3 P.M., and sunset. In this instance, Peter and John were on their way to the 3 P.M. prayer.

When we pray for divine appointments, sometimes God puts people in our paths who we can share with. The lame man asked for money, but God through Peter gave him something better—the use of his legs and a knowledge of Jesus. It was an incredible miracle as Peter took him by the right hand, helped him up, and the man began to walk and then jump around and praise God. So Peter took this opportunity to share more with the crowd who had gathered. Verses 11–13 state,

> They all rushed out in amazement to Solomon's Colonnade, where the man was holding tightly to Peter and John.
>
> Peter saw his opportunity and addressed the crowd. . . . "It is the God of Abraham, Isaac, and Jacob—the God of all our ancestors—who has brought glory to his servant Jesus by doing this" (NLT).

We, too, can pray and make plans as we trust in the Lord for opportunities to share Jesus.

Bible studies provide opportunities

Corleen and I conducted a Bible study at my home with a lady named Sandy for several months. Sandy, who owns rental houses, once mentioned that she had a poor tenant, adding, "She could use pictures for her walls and a few other items."

"Does this lady need a coffee table? My parents have one they don't use," I asked.

"Probably; I don't think she has one," responded Sandy.

Corleen added, "I have a picture or two at my home I could give."

The next day I picked up the coffee table, and Corleen brought me a huge picture to give away. The picture must have been six feet long by three feet tall. When I got home, I called Sandy, and we went over to deliver the table and picture to her tenant, Karen. Karen came out, and Sandy introduced me. As I opened up the van's rear hatch, I asked Karen, "Do you like this picture?"

"Yes, that is really nice. I like it."

We carried in the picture and the coffee table. Karen had a big blank wall that needed a picture that size. The coffee table filled the hole in the middle of the room, and I was so glad I brought it.

As we were walking out, I did not want to leave without a prayer or something, so I mentioned, "Karen, my friend Corleen and I found out about your need in a Bible study group with Sandy. And I just wanted you to know that we prayed for you." Karen looked at me intently while I talked and then asked, "What religion are you?"

"I'm a Christian first and then a Seventh-day Adventist," I responded. Instantly, she thrust out her hand and said in short, blunt sentences, "Baptized. Seventh-day Adventist. Year 2000." Then she confessed, "I haven't been back to the church since. I have backslidden, and I smoke."

"Well, He's a big God," I reassured her. "I'm sure He can handle it." I shared a little more of Jesus' love and asked about her background with Him. Then I asked, "Do you want to go back to church? There is one just down the street from you."

"I don't own a car," she responded.

"If you want to go, I will find someone to take you," I shared. I thought, *Is this ever a problem for God?* Karen, Sandy, and I took the opportunity to pray right then.

One of my friends attended that church so I called, and Karen started going to church again. God knew she was ready to come back to church and just needed someone to connect with her.

Sometimes God sharpens us

During one Monday morning prayer group in September 2003, I shared, "Two of my friends need prayer. One is really closed-minded, and another is too open-minded. I visited both of them within days of each other and now I really see the difference." I continued while the three other ladies stared at me, "The close-minded or conservative one makes statements such as, 'We never put our kids in Pathfinders because it's not good for children to go on campouts with the opposite sex.'

"The open-minded friend said, 'A friend of mine gave me a statue of a dragon to put in my house. He is from one of those Eastern religions and says this statue is a goddess of protection.' She asked me, 'Do you think that is OK to put in my house?'

" 'No,' I replied strongly. 'It reminds me of the nations that surrounded the Israelites in the Bible with all their idols.'

"She answered, 'But I have to think of this from his angle. He will be offended and hurt if I don't take it. If I had been born in his country, I would be his religion and it wouldn't matter.'

"We were walking between stores, and I decided not to argue anymore. Then we came to the bookstore. We started to pass by a book on witches, and I pointed to it, implying, *Hey, don't touch that one.* Seeing this as an invitation, she grabbed it, opened it, and started reading. 'They have interesting insights in here. Listen to this.' I was shocked. Apparently, I shock easily. 'No, I don't want to listen. I have witnessed demons behind the scenes and want no part of their ideas.' "

As I finished telling this to the prayer group, who had not made a comment yet, I grabbed my scripture promise book and said, "We need to claim a text for these two people." I opened the front of the book and scanned the table of contents while thinking, *If there is a text for the occasion, God usually helps me to see it.* The "Judgment–Criticism" section jumped out at me. The three ladies were still listening and watching me.

Uh-oh, I thought, *God might be trying to tell me something.* Turning to the page, I saw Romans 14:13: "Therefore let us not judge one another anymore, but rather resolve this, not to put a stumbling block or a cause to fall in our brother's way" (NKJV).[1]

"Lord, is this for me?" I said out loud, with the others still listening to me. "I wasn't intending to be judgmental."

As if in answer, a paraphrase of Galatians 6:1 at the bottom of the page jumped out at me. "When God allows us to see a fault in another, He is giving us a burden or a word of knowledge for that person. It is your opportunity to be an intercessor. Do not use this knowledge to stand in judgment or to criticize. Let the Holy Spirit do the convicting and sanctifying work that needs to be done because you prayed for him. God uses these occasions to teach us His ways and move us into maturity."[2]

I looked up at the ladies and said, "Well, thank You, Lord, for reminding me I'm an intercessor. When I get up to heaven, I'll probably find out many people were sending up earnest prayers for me also, because they thought I was way off."

Connections back east

About this time, Corleen received advertising for an event for the tenth anniversary of the *Women of Spirit* magazine. "What do you think about going to Hagerstown, Maryland, for this event?" Corleen asked while holding out the invitation for me to see.

"You know I love an adventure; let's go!" I said excitedly. My mind started to whirl about who all we could see at the same time. *My cousin Debi lives in Westminster, Maryland, and Georgia Shaffer lives in Pennsylvania, not far away,* I thought. So I continued, "And while we are there, we could see some other people too, like Georgia and my cousin Debi." Corleen's husband had a cousin nearby, so we prayed about it. Corleen called Ginger Church, the sales director for the magazine, and we signed up a few weeks later.

A couple of months later Ginger phoned us back to say, "You were the only two to sign up, so we had to cancel the event."

"We have already purchased our plane tickets," Corleen shared.

"Then you should come stay at my house, and I'll show you some interesting sights and show you around the Review and Herald campus."

We landed in Baltimore, Maryland, on April 22, 2004, rented a car, and went to Georgia's house first. We had a wonderful time with Georgia, enjoying her lovely flower garden and pond and some times of prayer. The next morning (also my fortieth birthday) Corleen and I were standing downstairs in Georgia's home. As I looked out the sliding glass door at the scenery, I thought back to how Georgia and I met because I fell off a bike, then how I flew across the country to attend CLASSeminar. Then two years later she came to the CLASSeminar Corleen and I sponsored in Women's Ministries and that same year Ron and I flew back to visit Georgia.

Here we are again. What will happen now?

"Corleen, can you come over here by the window?" I asked, then related what I was thinking. "What do you think will happen now?"

"I don't know, but God does. Let's pray about it," she replied in her usual response. While we were praying about Georgia, God said to me, *"I will bring her back into your life after seven years."*

"What!" My chin dropped, and I gasped. I was horrified at the thought that seven years had to pass by before something would happen.

"Corleen, God just said, 'I will bring her back into your life after seven years.' Do you know how long that is? What is going to happen in the meantime?" I started to feel a deep ache inside.

Corleen responded, "Oh, Diane, we'll keep so busy in Women's Ministries that seven years will pass by in no time." I was not convinced. We went up the stairs to eat breakfast, pray with Georgia, and say Goodbye. We drove to Gettysburg for some sightseeing, visited with Debi, and then spent some special time with Ginger Church.

God is always true to His word; and in April 2011, I felt overwhelmingly compelled to call Georgia. I was on vacation, so I talked myself into waiting. It was June when I felt compelled again, called, and left a message. A few days later she had an unexpected surgery and then another delay so she was not able to get back to me until August 24. On August 25, I became her long-distant assistant, and we are also prayer partners. It is very interesting how God orders our lives.

God even lines up a little girl

Several women were helping Corleen and me prepare our booth for camp meeting at the Gladstone, Oregon, campgrounds. It was the day before camp meeting was to begin. People were already there camping on the grounds. As lunch rolled around, Ginny and Corleen suggested we head to lunch, swinging by the bathroom first. I followed but did not go into the bathroom. Time passed. More time passed, and I began to wonder what was taking them so long. Then I began to be self-conscious. *People are going to wonder why I am standing here.* The thought occurred to me, *Maybe they left from a different door and forgot me.* I thought, *Who could forget me?* I looked around, but I did not feel compelled to leave. So I just stood there, thinking, *Every day I pray that I will be in the right place at the right time to help God's people. Surely I must be in the right place now.*

Just then I turned around and saw a man striding toward me holding on to a little girl around the age of six. In a split second, I noticed she was all dirty. He said, "There was a fight in the sandbox, and she has dirt in her eyes. I can't take her in the bathroom. Will you?"

That must hurt, I thought. She had big chunks of dirt plus sand in them. If I had been in her place, I would have been scared, crying, and probably wanted my mother. *Where is her mother?* I wondered.

As I was dabbing wet paper towels on her eyes and face, I started talking about camp meeting and how much fun it was going to be for her to learn more about Jesus. In Peter's opportunity story in Acts 3, while addressing the crowd, notice that he told them the "how-to." Peter did three things:

1. He told them who Jesus is (verse 13).
2. He gave them background information (verse 14).
3. He told them what they needed to do (verse 19).

So I said, while cleaning the little girl's eyes, "You are going to have so much fun learning about Jesus during your meetings."

Then I gave some background information. "You know it sure was a good thing I was standing there. I pray every day that God will put me in the right spot."

Obviously, this was not the time to say, "Do you, or don't you accept the gospel?" to a six-year-old girl. But there was a choice to make. "We need to go to a first-aid station and get eye drops for your eyes. Will that be OK with you? Your eyes will feel even better after that." She did not like it when she saw she had to sit back and hold her eyes open, but afterward I let her go back and play. However, God was not finished with that little girl.

Yes, Corleen admitted she did forget me and left through the other bathroom door. It was not the first time and probably not the last time. Yet, it did delay me to be in the right spot for the little girl.

Later that afternoon Corleen and I were walking when I saw the little girl standing beside a woman in a wheelchair. So I introduced myself and discovered this was her mother. She seemed unconcerned when I explained what happened earlier. The next day I saw them again outside the tent our booth was in. I walked over and invited them to see it. The mother gave a cursory glance at our booth and said, "Would you watch her while I go look for her brother?"

"Of course," I replied. Then my cell phone rang, and I left the girl with Ginny and Corleen.

"My brother called in with a prayer request," I said, stepping back to the group.

We gathered in a circle, inviting the little girl to join us, and we held her little hands. As we poured our prayers over Mark's request, all three of us also held up the little girl in our midst. God will accomplish mighty things through that little girl. Remember Revelation 5:8 says God holds our prayers in golden bowls in heaven: "Each one had a harp and they were holding golden bowls full of incense, which are the prayers of God's people." He will pour them out at the right time.

The letter

It was June 30, 2004, and I was left with instructions to declutter Corleen's files while she was on a trip. This sounded like great fun, since I hate clutter and can easily visualize organization. A few days prior to this, for three nights in a row, I had a dream about a lady named Paula.* The second time I had the dream I thought, *Because I keep thinking about Paula during*

---

* Paula is a pseudonym.

the day too, it must mean I'm supposed to pray for her. So I started praying for Paula while sorting through Corleen's files. Looking through files and taking out items to be thrown out took parts of three days. By midmorning on the third day, I was on to the files beginning with the letter *S*. I opened a file marked "Stories." I gasped inwardly as I looked. There on top was an envelope with Paula's return address. Dare I open it? It looked like a personal letter addressed to Corleen. She did say to go through her files, and this was in her files. The letter was dated almost ten years prior. Yes, I determined it was a God moment and God must want me to open it. It was a typed letter dated just after a Christian women's retreat. It read, "Thanks for the blessings of the retreat, it was truly healing. I have had some ups and downs in life: shame, hurt, times when I didn't want life to go on. . . . I know God has been there and touched me through people . . ." It went on.

I knew I needed to call Paula. I thought, *She must be really struggling and in the exact same place mentally as the day she wrote this letter.* I thought I remembered where she worked and reached her after the main office patched me through.

"Hi, Paula; how are you?" I asked.

"I'm fine; how are you?" she asked.

"Great," I responded, wondering why people always respond they are fine when they are not.

"I have been thinking about you," I continued. "In fact, since I keep thinking of you, I thought maybe you needed prayer, so I have been praying for you."

"Thank you," said Paula, "I could use the extra prayers. This weekend I went with some friends to the beach to relax and get rid of stress. I have been thinking about you, too, and wondered when the next time I would see you would be. Have you been playing tennis lately? I haven't seen you at the club."

"I have only gone once. I'll have to go again, maybe I'll see you," I remarked.

"That would be nice," Paula said.

"Paula," I continued, "I have been cleaning out files here at the office while Corleen has been gone."

"Oh, where has she gone?" Paula asked.

"She is on a three-week Reformation tour of England and Scotland. I'm sure she will learn lots of history. By the way, while cleaning files, I found a letter from you written to Corleen. I would like to read it to you." While

I read, I could feel the Holy Spirit's power and started to get choked up because I knew God was right on target with this.

When I finished reading, there was a small moment of silence, then Paula said, "That is right where I am now."

"I wondered," I responded. "God is usually right on about these things. I just want you to know that because God showed me your letter, He must really care about you and where you are right now, and He wants to see you through this."

"May I have a copy of that letter?" Paula asked.

"Of course, I'll send you one," I said.

I shared a verse that God gave me for her and prayed with her. I stand in awe of God and the ways He connects people. Galatians 6:9, 10 shares, "Let us not become weary in doing good, for at the proper time we will reap a harvest if we do not give up. Therefore, as we have opportunity, let us do good to all people, especially to those who belong to the family of believers."

Moments of Reflection:

1. Share a moment with friends, or journal a divine-intervention moment. Are you praying for these to happen?

2. Do you feel like God is lining up the events of your life with His will? Can you say that you trust Him with your future?

---

1. June Newman Davis, comp., *Scripture Keys for Kingdom Living* (Denver, CO: Scripture Keys Ministries, 1999), 93.

2. Ibid.

CHAPTER TWENTY

Who Is Driving? Where Are We Going?

"God is with you in everything you do."

—*Genesis 21:22*

Personally, I think exercise and motorcycle riding are relaxing. One day while riding, I saw a goat with his head sticking through some block-wire fencing. "Lord, that goat looks stuck. Someone needs to help him; send someone to help him," I prayed as I rode past. Almost an hour later, on my way back from the gym, there was the goat with his head still stuck in the fence. Seized by remorse that it was me who was supposed to help, I pulled over. Walking up to the goat, I reached around his head and yanked two directions on the wire, and he pulled his head out.

Another time when I left the gym, I jumped on to my motorcycle and lifted my hand to press the starter button, but my hand seemed frozen in position and would not push the starter. A thought occurred to me. *God thinks I forgot something. Mental checklist: I have my helmet on, my motorcycle boots, my motorcycle gloves. Exercise clothes are under the seat. What am I forgetting?* So I said, "Lord, what am I forgetting? I have my helmet, gloves, shoes; what?"

God encouraged, *"Ask Me to drive."*

"Oh," I said, "I'm sorry." You see, usually when I get on a motorcycle I ask God to drive. So I said, "Lord, You need to drive." I pressed the starter, backed up, headed out, and rounded a corner. A car pulled out from a stopped position next to the curb and drove right into me without hitting me. Somehow my motorcycle drove right around it. At the next stop sign, I shuddered, thinking, *How did I not get hit? What if I hadn't asked God to drive?* Please do not misunderstand me; I am not saying you will never get hit if you ask God to drive.

Mission, mission everywhere

When I was a child, I spent a week every summer with my grandmother during camp meeting, and one of the highlights was the money she gave me to spend in the bookstore. It was with awe and wonder that I stared at all the covers and titles of the books. The missionary stories always fascinated me, and I would choose several to take back to the tent to read. I prayed to become a missionary someday as my faith built on the stories of people who had gone before me to foreign lands. *So many of their prayers were answered, so many close calls, so many sacrifices made. What would it take to be like them?* I wondered.

Stormie Omartian, in her book *The Power of a Praying Wife*, says, "I've observed that people who have had actively praying parents seem to find their life's work early. Their careers may not take off immediately, but they have a sense of purpose and destiny that propels them in the right direction."[1] So it was that I had this inner longing for mission.

Early in 2005, I felt compelled to do a survey of the women at my church. One of the questions I posed was about short-term missions. "I would love to go on a short-term mission trip. I could help in these ways: _____." Out of twenty-two respondents, fourteen said they would be interested in a short-term mission trip. *Oh my,* I thought, *this needs to be a back-burner project.* However, God thought, *This will make good front-burner plans. Ring* went my phone a few days later. "We're doing a volunteer day, and we want to profile each ministry at the church with a booth," someone from the church called to say. Since I was the Women's Ministries coordinator at our church, I prayed and pondered this new idea. The thought came to me to make a handout that shared upcoming events and plans we were working on. So I wrote down plans and gave it to one of the ladies on my committee for her opinion. "I see you have the idea of a short-term mission trip on here. My husband and I coordinated a mission trip to Mexico once, and if you go there, I will come and be your cook," Melinda said.

I nearly fell over. "You will?"

God must want me to pursue this, I thought. The next day at the office I approached Karen in another department about ideas for places in Mexico. She used to work at the North Pacific Union Conference and helped organize many mission trips. Karen gave me a packet of information and a tape to watch of an organization that did building projects. This did not sound very exciting. My passion was to have an evangelistic series because I wanted to preach. (God had definitely worked a change in me since the Philippines!)

On Sabbath evening, I put the video in to watch and then held up the tape and said, "Lord, You know that I am willing, but anyone can work on a building. Is this really what You want me to do?" Then I waited; no response. Sometimes God delays His answer.

The next morning I was flipping channels on the television and happened upon the Crystal Cathedral's *Hour of Power*. Right then a man said, "So I went to Wall Street and told the guys there I wanted them to come to Africa with me to plant gardens. The people there need gardens. The men said, 'You want us to go all the way to Africa just to plant a garden?'

" 'Yes, and I want you to put three thousand dollars of your own money toward it also.' " Next they flashed the man's name on the screen: Bruce Wilkinson. Now I really paid attention because I remembered his book *The Prayer of Jabez*. He continued to tell about how a whole team of people went with him to Swaziland with the goal to plant 10,000 gardens. On the first day, they planted 500; the next day 1,100; and by Thursday, Bruce decided to stay in his hotel and fast and pray. In the end, they had planted 12,800 gardens. People came up to him and said, "You know we didn't think God cared about us down here in Swaziland, but then He sent you, so now we know He cares." I was choked up now. *This is incredible!* I thought. *God just spoke to me. If these people could go all the way to Africa just to plant a garden, surely I could be helpful in Mexico. I am supposed to go to Mexico!* That was in April 2005.

Melinda was visiting the office a few days later and mentioned, "Why don't we shoot for the second week in May next year?" It sounded good to me to have a whole year to plan. Consequently, I called the organization for more facts and to ask about the date. They wanted a minimum of about fourteen people and two thousand dollars for materials. So I started advertising for people. Months went by, and only a few people seemed interested.

Soon it was October, and one day we received a call in Women's Ministries from Sue Patzer in the North Pacific Union Conference office. She was organizing a group of fifty teams to go to Bolivia in March 2006. Each team would preach a one-week series, and then the next two weeks her husband, Jere, would preach to all the churches in a huge gymnasium. Sue wanted Corleen and me to get some teams together. *Would it be worth it to go all that way? What about my Mexico trip?* I wondered.

As if God knows exactly what we need to answer our questions, the next day I read an article in the *Adventist Review* about people who traveled three and four days, walking and carrying all of their luggage and children to get to a series of meetings. *If they can travel all that way, surely I am able to. How can I not go? I wouldn't have to walk. I would go by plane.* Sensing God wanted me to do both trips, I had a dilemma: I needed people for Mexico and a roommate for Bolivia.

Bolivia

December soon arrived, and I was worried about details for the upcoming trips. My friend, Sandy, came with me to a Christmas brunch, and on the drive there, she said she would go to Bolivia with me. Later she changed her mind, deciding to go to Mexico instead. This was fantastic that she wanted to come. It is interesting that God encourages us along the way, yet sometimes waits till the very last minute to tweak details. I kept holding on to the promise in Genesis 21:22, "God is with you in everything you do," and tried not to worry.

Corleen and I coordinated with a lady named Donna Griffith on an event called Prayer Quest for February 2006 in a southern Oregon church. On the Tuesday after the event was over, Donna phoned to talk to both of us.

Donna said enthusiastically, "I'm just bursting with the blessings from the weekend. And it will feel unusual to not talk to you two every day. I'll miss that. But I know that Diane will find me something else to do, she always does."

We hung up with Donna, and I went back to sit at my desk and work on getting the Prayer Quest details in order to put the information file away. Suddenly, a thought came into my mind that God must have put there. *I know Donna is short on funds. I wonder if Donna would go to Bolivia if Women's Ministries bought her a ticket.* So I said out loud to Corleen, "Hey, Corleen, we ought to see if Donna would come to Bolivia with us if we bought her a ticket."

Corleen replied, "We might be able to do that."

"May I call her and offer?"

"Sure," she replied, "but I think I remember Donna saying that her husband did not want her to go to Bolivia."

I picked up the phone. "Donna," I asked, "are you sitting down? Would you go to Bolivia with us if we purchased an airline ticket for you?"

"Are you serious? I was just praying, and I was so pumped from Prayer Quest that I told God I wanted to do evangelism for Him. I did not expect an answer immediately. I have to call my husband, Mel."

Moments later she called back. "I can't believe it, but he said Yes. He said,

'If they are willing to buy you a ticket, then you have to go.' " Donna would be my roommate for Bolivia.

One plan down, one needed

On March 4, while on my way to church, with a week left before Bolivia and two months before Mexico, I prayed, "Lord, please block anyone that is not meant to go on the mission trip to Mexico and give me who You need to go. You know what is best. You know what we will be doing, and I don't. Please, may Your will be done."

Walking into church, Melinda greeted me at the door. "My daughter has just been diagnosed with cancer. I probably won't be able to go on the trip. I want to be with her if she is undergoing surgery and chemotherapy."

"Let's pray right now for her," I said. Then I prayed earnestly with Melinda for her daughter that God's will be done.

Sitting down by my mother later, she startled me: "I've been thinking, I may not be able to go to Mexico. My doctor wanted me to be careful since my surgery about not catching any strange bugs."

That afternoon I prayed, "Lord, You know, we only have five people for sure now. That's not enough to build a building. Maybe we are meant to hold an evangelistic series in the next town from where we were building. Valle de la Trinidad is only five miles away. I'm not complaining, but You need to give some direction."

No reply from God.

"OK, then, I'm going to read the Bible now." Glancing down, my eyes fell on John 4:39, where I had the Bible open: "Many of the Samaritans from that town believed in him because of the woman's testimony."

Oh my. My mind whirled. *I need to switch plans to doing an evangelistic series, and there is no time to lose.* I called God's five people, and they were fine with helping with a series instead of a building.

Monday arrived, and I was to leave on Wednesday for Bolivia. Now with two days left, I needed to confirm a place in Mexico for a team. I was lamenting to Corleen about what to do when she said, "Dial Lois, and we can pray with her too." There was only fifteen minutes till Ron came to take me to a tax appointment. Corleen's phone rang, and she answered, so I called Lois by myself. Lois replied, "Diane, God gave you the evangelism idea for a reason. Why don't you call the conference that has Valle de la Trinidad in it and ask them if you can come?"

Suddenly, I was like a house on fire. To locate a phone number, first I called the General Conference and asked for the Adventist Mission Department. They transferred me, but I reached a voice message. I called them back again and asked if there was another person in that department and reached another voice mail. We had a book with all of the Adventist conferences in the world listed, and I grabbed it. "Lord, which conference am I looking for?" I was flipping through the book quickly and said again, "Lord, I need Your help. Show me where to look in this book."

Suddenly, I saw the Southeastern California Conference and thought, *That has to be close; maybe they will know.* I called and asked if there was a pastor in the Valle de la Trinidad area.

"Oh, yes, there are five churches in the area, but you should call the Baja California Conference. Try this number."

So I called the Baja California Conference, and a woman answered in Spanish. I asked, "Does anyone speak English?"

"Yes, I speak English," the lady replied, switching to English. "There are five churches in the Valle de la Trinidad area. Here's the number, but the pastor doesn't speak English."

Oh, great, I thought. Just then Ron walked in the door, and I explained what was happening as he urged, "We need to go now."

I responded, "Tell me exactly how many minutes do I have if we just barely make it to the tax appointment?"

"Ten minutes," he replied.

"Well, that's enough time to fix this whole thing," I asserted. So I picked up the phone and called. The first person that answered was a man, and I asked, "Is there anyone there who speaks English?" Silence. I thought, *Maybe this is the pastor.*

Soon a woman got on the line. "Hello."

"Hi, I'm Diane Pestes, and I would like to come down to your town to do an evangelistic series, and there are five people who are really interested in coming to help also. They could help with health talks or any other projects you need, perhaps repairing something. We can come May 14–21." I paused for a breath, and the lady spoke, "Oh, that would be wonderful. You can stay in the dorm, and we have a medium-sized kitchen with two refrigerators that you can use and eat in the cafeteria. We will go with your plan and have interpreters you can use."

Suddenly, it hit me. *What did she just say? Did she say Yes? Did God just answer all of my prayers?* Emotions started to creep in like I was going to cry, but I am not a crying type of person.

Oh my! God did want us to go to this town! "Please tell me your name," I said, realizing I did not even know who I was talking to.

"I'm Gwendoly, and I'm the secretary at the school here. Oh, we have had groups come before, but they have always done community service–type projects. You should talk to the pastor here. He will want to know you are coming. Here, I'll give you his number."

"Thank you so much, Gwendoly. I would talk to you some more, but I have to rush off to a meeting. Goodbye."

Two hours later I called the pastor. A woman answered in Spanish. I asked for the pastor in English. "Oh, just a momento; momento, please." Then I heard banging like she was hitting the outside of her house and shouting, "Susanna, Susanna."

A woman named Susanna got on the line instead of the pastor. By this time, I did not feel as rushed and choleric, so I explained a little more how God had inspired our team to want to be of help. "That would be wonderful," she related. "We are excited you are coming." Then she interpreted to the pastor's wife, adding, "What is your number? I'll have him call you back."

On my way home that evening, my cell phone rang, and a lady said, "Hi, I go to the Mount Tabor church, and I saw your ad about the mission trip. I know I'm calling too late, but when my daughter and I saw the ad we really wanted to go. Do you have enough people?"

Thinking quickly, I said, "Well, yes, but we have actually changed the emphasis from building to holding an evangelistic series."

She replied, "We would love to help with an evangelistic series. I have been in women's ministries for thirty years, so I can talk on those topics, and my daughter and I love putting on children's ministries meetings."

"That's it," I said. "You and your daughter can do the children's ministries meetings. How wonderful! Oh, by the way, what did you say your name is?" "Polly Johnson, and my daughter's name is Becky Johnson."

When I hung up, the phone rang again, and it was the pastor confirming that he wanted us to come.

Whew! All of the pieces were in place as well as they could be. The next day I was off to Bolivia. Only God could put the pieces together so quickly at the last minute. When we ask God to take charge, we can rest assured we will get to the destination. Ephesians 3:7 shares, "I became a servant of this gospel by the gift of God's grace given me through the working of his power." Thank the Lord He can be with us in everything we do.

Moments of Reflection:

1. Share with a group one of the passions God has given you. (The people who are listening should not offer any comments other than, "Praise the Lord, God has given you a great talent.") Go around the circle, giving each person an opportunity to share their God-given passions. Then pray for each person, that God will use their talents mightily for Him.

2. When God puts someone or something right in front of you, you are the one God is asking to step in and give help.

---

1. Stormie Omartian, *The Power of a Praying Wife* (Eugene, OR: Harvest House Publishers, 1997), 51.

CHAPTER TWENTY-ONE

We "Go" by Faith

By faith Abraham, when called to go . . . , obeyed and went,
even though he did not know where he was going.
—*Hebrews 11:8*

What did I get myself into? I questioned. Usually bold and eager to head out on an adventure, sometimes I hesitate when the actual day comes. *This is for real. I'm going a long way away without my husband, Ron,* I thought. I was very quiet on the drive to the airport. Corleen and Paul were sitting in the backseat. *Well, at least my prayer partner is going with me,* I thought. At the terminal counter, I found out Corleen would be on another plane, so suddenly it felt like I was going by myself. However, in Denver, most of the teams would be on the same flight to Bolivia. When something bothers me, it is usually a sign that the situation needs prayer. So I started praying, "Lord, please guide these flights. You have to be in control, and get all of the teams there safely." It's probably a good thing that I felt this way because it caused me to pray most of the way to Denver. There was a snowstorm in Denver, which delayed our departure, and then they deiced the plane before we headed to yet another plane in Mexico City. We landed in Mexico City long past the departure time of our connecting flight. Our leaders passed instructions back through the airplane: "They held our plane, quickly get off, go get a stamp in your passport, and come back to the terminal."

Great reception

"I'm in Bolivia . . . praise the Lord." These were my words in an e-mail home on March 9, 2006. "We had quite the reception at the airport. It seems everyone turned out: the Pathfinders, the young adults, the adults. They pinned tiny decorative pins on us and gave us each a two-inch by four-inch satchel that they hung around our necks. 'To keep your money in,' they said. I'm a little dizzy from lack of sleep, but fine other than that. They told us we have a 3:00 P.M. meeting for orientation, then tomorrow we go to the market for food and water."

My mind let their last statement sink in: *We wait until tomorrow for food and water? What do we do today?* As we walked toward our rooms, I spotted a little café. *OK, I can grab a bite there if I get desperate,* I thought.

The next day arrived, and Donna and I walked toward the bus taking the group to a grocery store in the city. Turning toward Corleen, "You're not going?" I asked her.

"No, I want to go with my driver, Hugo, to visit my new church. This is the time that works best for him," she said. Corleen had brought along a water filter she said I could use, so I did not need to buy bottled water. However, I knew it would be too expensive to eat all my meals at the outdoor café downstairs from our room. So, along with Donna and a few others, I boarded the bus.

Traffic is very different in Bolivia: minimal signage, many roundabouts with no one yielding, and an overall lack of safety features. Several miles into our trip, our local driver went through a red light. Donna was sitting on the other side of our van. Out my window, I saw a driver in a jeep type of vehicle coming toward me fast. There was only a split second to think, *I'm a goner.* My adrenaline spiked with no time to even move to the other side. Inwardly, I was sucking in air, fully expecting to die. The driver stopped two inches outside my window. *How did that happen?* My mind raced. *Did an angel stop the vehicle, or are Bolivians that good at driving that they can stop two inches from you?* "Donna, did you see that?"

She had. "I'm shaking too!" she replied. It was going to be a hard experience to forget. We found several food items to take back to our room, though it ended up that we never used any of it. At the end of our trip, we gave the food to the lady who cleaned our apartment. Turns out we had a lack of faith that God would provide.

We were amazed and appreciative that the group in the apartment next to us kept giving us their leftovers. A number of students from the Montana Conference had come to build a church, and their cook made huge batches of food for all of them. God really provided for us between the food next door and Corleen, who made connections with people who went to the market daily because she wanted fresh lettuce every day. I can still picture her soaking lettuce in bleach water and washing lentils.

The people and the meetings

After my "near-death" experience, I questioned why I came so far but not for long. When you meet the wonderful people, the reasons all come back. Hebrews 11:8 talks about Abraham's faith in going from his home. "By faith Abraham, when called to go . . . , obeyed and went, even though he did not know where he was going." Oswald Chambers comments on this in his book *My Utmost for His Highest,* "One of the most difficult questions to answer in Christian work is, 'What do you expect to do?' You don't know what you are going to do. The only thing you know is that God knows what He is doing. Continually examine your attitude toward God to see if you are willing to 'go out' in every area of your life, trusting in God entirely. It is this attitude that keeps you in constant wonder, because you don't know what God is going to do next."[1]

Louise, my teammate for the meetings, did the children's stories, health blurbs, and kept the technical details in order. One day our friendly driver, Waldo, picked us up during a huge rainstorm. When it rains in Bolivia, some streets flood because you are driving on sand with no drainage ditches. Water shot up the sides past our window, and cars stalled all around us. If you stall, no one can come to help, because the water is too high in places, and unsanitary items make the water unsafe to walk in. Some people live in cardboard boxes along the road, adding to the sanitation problems.

Arriving at the church, I noticed an elder using a squeegee broom to push water out a side door. It seemed to come in just as fast, and the roof dripped directly over the spot where the projector usually sat.

The people were already coming into "our" church named La Colorada. I could not understand many of them as they tried to speak to me. But they always hugged me, kissed me on both cheeks, and chattered away like I could understand them. As I went to the center of the room, I motioned everyone to come where the water visibly fell from the ceiling. *"Vamos a orar,"* I said in my best Spanish and folded my hands together—meaning "We pray now."

Misha, one of our interpreters said, "Four weeks ago we had so much rain people died." Horrified at the thought, I could easily visualize the people who lived in the cardboard boxes suffering from the rain. Glancing at the elder to see if he had any comments, he motioned I should pray, so I did, "Lord, we praise You for our safe arrival; however, please be with those out in this storm, protect them, and bring them also to the meetings. We need You to stop the rain so we can have the meeting. You know computer equipment is very sensitive. Thank You for Your help, amen." We moved in faith and set up the equipment away from the leak, and soon the rain stopped.

Come close to people

Ernestine and Mark Finley share in their book *Light Your World for God*, "Jesus cared for people. He cared about their heartaches. He always got close enough to people to know what their needs were. . . . Jesus was always interested in the people around him. He was asking, 'What are you seeking? What are your longings? What needs do you have? I am interested in meeting them.' "[2]

Misha frequently put his hand to the side of his mouth, and one day I asked, "Are you in pain?"

"Yes, it hurts most of the time. I'm going to a dentist soon, and he will pull my tooth."

"Isn't there anything else that can be done besides pulling your tooth?" I asked.

"No money. I don't have any money to fix it. Many people just pull their teeth," he shared. Misha was only in his twenties, and I thought, *At this rate, he will have no teeth thirty years from now.* I had noticed people with missing teeth. Horrified at pulling a tooth that could be fixed in America, I said, "You know I could anoint you, and we could see if God fixes your tooth."

"No, ma'am, no anointing. That's for people who are dying," he replied.

"It's not just for people who are dying," I responded but realized his mind was made up. I said, "Well, then let's just have a regular prayer about it." This seemed agreeable to him, so we had a quick prayer and then he went home for the evening. The next day and through the rest of our trip he never complained of tooth pain, and he said it had been healed!

Baptism

"When are you going to make a call for baptism?" Misha asked one night after the meeting. I answered, "I'll pray and ask the Lord about it." Misha was eager for people to make decisions, and he must have been compelled by the Lord because two days later God whispered an unmistakable, *"Tonight,"* to me. Near the end of my sermon, I shared, "If you believe God will restore truth to His people in the last days, raise your hand. And if you desire to follow all the truth God has for you now, raise your hand. And if you would like to say, 'Yes, Jesus, I want to be baptized soon,' raise your hand." There were some hands, and Misha and I became excited. What a blessing to be part of connecting people to the Lord Jesus.

Shawn Boonstra, the director for *It Is Written,* led an evangelistic series in Portland once, and I attended one of the planning meetings where he shared five points for being successful.

This is my paraphrase:

1. Jesus ministers to the multitudes.
2. Go find those God is converting. You will not have to convince them.
3. Explain the Scriptures to them.
4. Tell them what you know of Jesus personally.
5. They will obtain a rich experience.

Sharing the gospel in a nutshell.

Injured girl

One night, after I finished shaking hands, I went back to get my computer when a woman ran up excitedly, speaking in Spanish and pointing at me. Misha, who overheard her words, swiftly came up, "We need you in the back; please come." I looked at Louise.

"I'll grab the projector and computer," she said, as if reading my thoughts. Never sure what God is doing next, I moved forward while praying quietly. There were two little rooms in the back of the church. As I approached, I heard a crying woman in a room. She was sitting in a chair, holding a young girl about eight years old. The girl looked unconscious, and the elder beckoned me toward two small pillows on the concrete floor in front of the woman.

Misha said, "A dog bit her, very bad. You pray."

"Why didn't they go to the hospital?" I asked.

"No money, just pray," he responded. What a foreign concept to think the hospital is not an option even in life-threatening issues! The elder and I knelt to pray. Knowing Jesus was all I had, I began, "Lord, all we have is You, and You can heal. Please heal this young child in Jesus' name like it never happened." I forget what else I said. The elder prayed in Spanish. The woman stood up, and I started to put my arm around her shoulder. She fled the room, but not before I caught a glimpse of the child. Her eyes opened, and she looked at me. As I began to gasp, "She's healed!" the woman was already halfway out the door.

When I got to the meeting the next night, I said to Misha, "What happened to the girl who was bitten by the dog?"

"She's right there," he said, pointing to a girl who was running around. I was not surprised. "Our God is great, so strong, and so mighty, there's nothing our God cannot do." So goes the song and my testimony. What a praise!

Other unusual blessings

One night Louise and I handed out tiny one-by-two-inch felt "Bibles" to the kids with the words *Santa Biblica* on the front and a little picture inside with a verse. One group took a lot of felts to their church ladies and reported that a lady started crying because she had been praying for felts for three years.

All too soon our time with the La Colorada church ended, and the follow-up meetings with Jere Patzer started. Four thousand people were there the first day, and it swelled from there. The meetings were broadcast by satellite all over South America, Central America, and places in Miami.

Taya, a former Bolivian rock star, gave her life to the Lord at a previous evangelistic series. She started singing Christian music and now sang at these meetings. Taya worked at the Bolivian Adventist media center in Cochabamba, and she wanted to film Corleen and me making lunch. It took a long time for the necessary basics: if you want to drink water, you must filter it; if you want fresh vegetables, you must wash them first, then soak them twenty minutes in an iodine (easily obtained in Bolivia) or bleach solution; if you want cooked lentils, you must filter and wash out the small fragments of rocks and other debris, then soak and cook them; if you want fresh laundry, you must wash one shirt at a time in the little laundry tub that holds about two shirts, then hang it to dry in another room with a drain in the floor.

Ever think you do not have enough clothes? While visiting an orphanage run by the Adventist Development and Relief Agency (ADRA), Donna and I learned that their most pressing need was T-shirts and underwear. The homeless boys they rescued only had one pair of underwear; so we sent new packages of underwear to the orphanage.

Sabbath blessings

Our last full day in Bolivia was a Sabbath. All of the people from the churches that had held meetings were gathered in the Sunny Loom Auditorium for a last meeting. Hundreds of people were lined up to be baptized—people who decided they could not live without Jesus.

Words cannot express what a blessing it is to be a part of connecting people to Jesus. I now long for my heavenly home to reconnect with these dear people again. Hebrews 11:15, 16 counsels us to look forward, "If they had been thinking of the country they had left, they would have had opportunity to return. Instead, they were longing for a better country—a heavenly one. Therefore God is not ashamed to be called their God, for he has prepared a city for them." We can be excited about this!

Moments of Reflection:

1. In the conversations you have with others, do you recognize opportunities for prayer?

2. Take the time to read Hebrews 11:8–16, and write a letter to God or share your thoughts with your group.

3. Do you believe God will restore truth to people in the last days? Do you desire to follow all of the truth God has for you now? Raise your hand. Would you like to say, "Yes, Jesus, I want to be baptized *soon*"? Raise your hand. If you raised your hand, please do not hesitate. Take your phone, call your pastor or look one up, and tell the pastor the Holy Spirit is prompting you to be baptized.

---

1. Oswald Chambers, "January 2: Will You Go Out Without Knowing?" in *My Utmost for His Highest* (Grand Rapids, MI: Discovery House Publishers, 1992).

2. Ernestine and Mark Finley, *Light Your World for God* (Fallbrook, CA: Hart Research Center, 2002), 108.

CHAPTER TWENTY-TWO

How Faith Turns Into Action

"You are the salt of the earth."

—*Matthew 5:13*

O h, Diane, have faith. Just wait; you are soon going to be busier than ever!" Julie assured me in 1999. Little did she know she was a prophetess. Hebrews 11:1 shares, "Now faith is confidence in what we hope for and assurance about what we do not see."

The online encyclopedia *Wikipedia* said, "The word *faith* is often used as a synonym for *hope, trust,* or *belief.*"[1] Sometimes friends can be faith for us. When faith becomes real for us, it looks like this: belief equals faith and action. For example, we can believe a plane can take us to Florida; but if we are too scared to get on the plane, then we do not have the faith to go with our belief. "Simply to say 'I believe in God' means very little if it is merely coming from the lips and not from the heart. People can, and do, say that they 'believe' in God, but their lives never change at all. . . . True faith, dependence/reliance/trust, in God reveals itself in our actions, our thought life, and our priorities."[2] For example, I believe Jesus died on the cross to save me from my sins and give me eternal life. My faith in this leads me to help others in ways I think God is showing me that will further His kingdom.

A few years after our trip to the Philippines, one day at the office, Corleen and I received an e-mail from Romulo, our Philippine correspondent. He wanted five hundred dollars to purchase a car. We had taken up offerings for his projects before and sent him large boxes numerous times filled with supplies. Now I thought, *All that, and he wants more? Where are we going to get five hundred dollars more? How can we provide everything for this man?* It is a good thing we do not always share our thoughts. As I calmed down, the car-need idea would not leave my mind. That night I opened my wallet, grabbed all I had—a sum total of three dollars—put it in an envelope, and labeled it "Philippine car." Holding it up before the Lord, I said, "OK, Lord, I believe You are going to do something special for Romulo. Please provide the rest of the funds."

Several days later a ten-year-old boy and his mother walked into our office. He was carrying his piggy bank and set it on my desk. His mother said, "We have read in your newsletter that you send money to the Philippines. A few days ago my son suddenly felt compelled to bring you what he has saved so far. We couldn't come until today, and he doesn't know how much it is. But we can count it together." It came to $197.00.

The day after that Corleen brought in three hundred dollars, stating, "Can you believe I put a Christmas one hundred dollar bill in a drawer for three years in a row and forgot about it?" I decided I better not comment and bit my tongue. It was incredible how God pulled together exactly five hundred dollars, not a penny more or less. So Romulo got his car because I acted on faith with action and held out three dollars and a prayer; because a ten-year-old boy acted on faith to keep saving for something special, answered the Spirit when prompted, and gave all he had; and because God saved Corleen's money for the right time, and then she gave what she had.

Belief becomes faith and action

We can have belief that something can happen, but we need the faith and action to pick up the phone, get out of the house, put the money in a jar, and claim it for whatever mission project or goal we are planning. Is God prompting you? Pray about it. Form a plan, and get moving in a direction. My good friend Ione Richardson used to tell me, "If you don't put yourself out there, God can't lead you in a direction by either blocking you from going forward or moving obstacles out of your way so you can go forward." God will bless you. Say with me, "I do believe; help me overcome my unbelief!" (Mark 9:24).

I like to think that I am bold. But some of the stories of the Reformers and people in the Bible are much more astounding. However, we, too, can ask for a greater measure of God's Holy Spirit. John 3:34 says, "For God gives the Spirit without limit." Jesus' name gives us authority, peace, and eternal life, to name a few things. What would we do without Jesus?

Peter and John used Jesus' name to heal someone in Acts 4: "When they saw the courage of Peter and John and realized that they were unschooled, ordinary men, they were astonished and they took note that these men had been with Jesus" (verse 13). What was the source of their power? They used what they had—Jesus' name. Acts 2:42–46 shares that the early church enjoyed these four things:

1. They devoted themselves to teaching and reading the Scriptures.
2. They had fellowship.
3. They broke bread together.
4. They prayed.

The last part of Peter's and John's prayer in Acts 4:29–31 states,

"Now, Lord, consider their threats and enable your servants to speak your word with great boldness. Stretch out your hand to heal and perform signs and wonders through the name of your holy servant Jesus."

After they prayed, the place where they were meeting was shaken. And they were all filled with the Holy Spirit and spoke the word of God boldly.

How many of them? All were filled. If you would like to turn your belief into faith and action, pray for the Holy Spirit.

Hold on to faith, despite appearances

It is easy to sit in a comfortable chair and read about the adventures of others, but it is another thing to get on a plane or rent a car and drive over the border into a third world country. So I was not surprised that Ron did not want to go to Mexico. He did, however, fly with me to San Diego a few days ahead of the Mexico trip to help me get supplies and visit some sights—but he did not want to go on a mission trip.

On Sunday, May 14, 2006, a taxi arrived early to take Ron to the airport to go home. He said a quick prayer with me and left. Then I knelt down and reviewed with the Lord what He had accomplished up to this point and asked for His blessing. A verse that I had claimed for the year came to my mind, Isaiah 30:21: "Whether you turn to the right or to the left, your ears will hear a voice behind you, saying, 'This is the way; walk in it.' " It would prove to be literal that day.

Sandy came over to my room, and we also prayed and then drove to the airport to pick up the rest of the team: Ken and Welky Hoffman, Russell Finch, Connie Michelsen, and Polly and Becky Johnson. Polly and Becky did not arrive on their flight or so I thought, and after searching and searching, I called Corleen for prayer, "I've lost part of the team!"

"What?" she responded, assuming the worst and sharing a prayer. Moments later Polly called to say they were in a different terminal than originally planned. We headed to the border with no time to lose. I did not want us to be in the middle of the desert at nightfall; instead, I planned to be at our destination, Valle de la Trinidad, Baja, California—a town of about five hundred people seemingly in the middle of nowhere.

"We're across the border?" I questioned out loud as I drove one van, and Ken drove another behind me. You would think there would be a sign moments before you are about to cross. No! Nada! Nothing! Then a split second later, three road choices appeared in front of me: straight, left, or right. "Isaiah 30:21," I said out loud in a split second and chose straight. This soon proved to dash my hopes because we veered around a long corner and headed directly into what looked like the middle of Tijuana. And I thought driving in Bolivia was bad. I had never seen bumper-to-bumper traffic like this! *Since I'm the one driving, at least I know when I'm pressing the brake!* Rolling down my window, I hollered out to traffic going the other way, "Is this the way to the beach?"

Violent shaking of arms and hands. "No. Turn around; go back!"

Rolling up my window and turning toward Russell in the passenger seat beside me, I said, "They're wrong, I know it." Somehow hearing someone say, "Turn around," kicked in my "I know our God is helping us" defenses. "Russell, would you roll down your window and ask someone out your window, please?" I asked. Russell's question brought great smiles and affirmation. At ease now, we soon broke through what turned out to be a small corner of the city and found the scenic ocean-view toll road to Ensenada.

Love in action

After a brief stop at Costco for fresh produce, we arrived an hour before nightfall at the Valle de la Trinidad Church and Covatri Seventh-day Adventist School. Gwendoly, the school's secretary, came out to greet us. She was very sweet and showed us our accommodations: a dorm with cots, one working toilet, a sink with only cold water, and a shower with only hot water!

The next morning after breakfast, devotions, and prayers with the others, we sprang into action. Ken and Russell set to work on fixing items and painting the bathrooms at the school. Connie and Sandy took over the school's cafeteria to make food for our group. Polly and Becky sorted through their Vacation Bible School supplies for the meetings. Pastor Jaime Vasquez Diaz, Welky, and I went to view the church and talk about the meetings.

Meetings blessed

That night God blessed us with forty children in the Vacation Bible

School and twenty adults in the church. Several people thought Sandy was a nurse after her health talk, even though she read her notes as Susanna interpreted. Sandy said, "It's amazing how they all pile into the back of a pickup to come hear about Jesus—with no car seats for the kids!" The next day Connie gave a talk about dental health to the kids in the school and an orphanage nearby, and then the locals wanted to take her to talk to welfare mothers. "Wait, I want to go with you," Susanna said and jumped into the car with them, holding Sandy's notes about blood pressure from the night before. This turned out to be another God moment because they were told young mothers would be at the event, but elderly women showed up instead. "How many of you have high blood pressure?" Susanna asked. Every hand went up, and Connie proceeded to talk about the issue, with many people asking questions afterward. Connie was overjoyed that her talks went so well because she did not think of herself as a public speaker. As she believed she could make a difference, her faith turned into action that made a difference.

The ladies from our group also visited an orphanage, and we saw how thrilled the people were with health information. One mother lamented, "My children won't eat what I fix them for supper. What should I do to keep them from wanting to go into town instead?"

"What are you fixing them for supper?" Connie asked. It turns out many mothers were fixing the same meal every night. Connie shared about variety.

One of the mothers asked, "Can you make meal plans for us?"

Polly and Becky jumped in to help with the plans because Connie was so busy during the day.

It takes everyone to make a team

"I feel awful, and Susanna might have to interpret," Welky, my translator, whispered one evening just before we stood to speak.

"Are you going to make it?" I asked.

"I don't know, I'll try," she replied.

"I'll be praying," I shared while thinking, *I guess we talk until she says differently.* Then we stood to speak. When we got to our dorm later, I asked, "Did you eat anything different today?"

"Well"— a slight hesitation—"Ken and I had some ice cream in town."

"Please don't do that again," I advised.

"I need to lie down," she replied.

"Wait a moment, let's pray first. Everyone please gather around Welky. We need to have a prayer." Turning back to Welky, I added, "It is nighttime, and I don't want anything happening to you in the night because we don't have a hospital here. All we have is charcoal and prayer." I had a short prayer. She looked at me, "It scares me when God answers so quickly! The pain is gone. I'm well."

I replied, "All praise to the Lord. Thank You, Lord." Welky never felt sick again nor did anyone else in the group the rest of the time.

Faith and prayer relieve anxiety

One night when we entered the dorm, Polly found a black widow spider and a tarantula. Russell stomped on both. This was not the first deadly bug encounter. My e-mail home the next day read, "With our open windows, I'm trying not to think about this and claim Psalm 91 instead or I would sleep in the car."

Charles Spurgeon says, "Worldly cares are frequent and most mischievous hindrances to prayer. . . . To receive everything from God's hands and to trust everything in God's hands is a happy way of living and very helpful to prayer. . . . Faith gives peace, and peace leaves the soul clear for prayer. But when care comes in, it confuses the mind and puts the heart away from pleading."[3]

The blessings

One morning during our devotions, prayers, and fellowshiping time, I shared, "It looks like we will have some money left over from this trip. I know that Pastor Jaime has shared they could use 3ABN and Hope Channel for their church and school." Everyone thought it was a good idea, and we made a presentation of $250. This was enough to cover their satellite dish and enable the viewing of Christian programming.

We were thrilled that, of the twenty people attending the adult meetings, three raised their hands for baptism at a later date. All the expense, time, and small discomforts pale in comparison to new friends who have joy in Christ now and throughout eternity. What a God-blessed week we had. Like a ripple in a pond, the influence of each person on the trip will keep spreading till Jesus comes.

Making a difference is sharing Jesus, praying with others, and moving forward with bigger plans than you can accomplish unless God intervenes. Matthew 5:13 says, "You are the salt of the earth. But if the salt loses its saltiness, how can it be made salty again? It is no longer good for anything, except to be thrown out and trampled underfoot." Have you ever made bread or oatmeal without salt? It's not good. Job 6:6 says, "Is tasteless food eaten without salt?"

Jeremiah talks about Jerusalem, the capital city and center of worship for Judah. God wanted to spare the city if just one good person could be found. Jeremiah 5:1 says,

"Go up and down the streets of Jerusalem,
   look around and consider,
   search through her squares.
If you can find but one person
   who deals honestly and seeks the truth,
   I will forgive this city."

Talk about the power of one person's influence! How can we be salt and make a difference? The book *Becoming a Contagious Christian* says,

It could be that Jesus meant for salt to symbolize the idea of creating thirst. When Christians are in tune with the Holy Spirit, and when they live in their world with a sense of purpose, and with peace and joy, this often creates a spiritual thirst in the people around them. . . .

When Christians live out their faith with authenticity and boldness they put a little zing into a sometimes bland cup of soup.[4]

"You are the salt of the earth" (Matthew 5:13). We are the salt, and by faith we believe we can make a difference, then we pray, form a plan, and start moving toward the goal.

Moments of Reflection:

1. Share with your group or journal how being *salt* this week has touched you. Did you have belief with action? Did you use Jesus' name for success?

2. Are you taking moments for personal devotions, small-group Bible study, prayers, and reflection? We can only share Christ as we ourselves get to know Him better.

3. Converse with others in your group about the balance of taking care of yourself and sharing Jesus.

1. *Wikipedia*, s.v. "Faith," modified February 3, 2015, http://en.wikipedia.org/wiki/Faith.

2. Robert Driskell, "What Is the Difference Between Faith and Belief? A Bible Study," What Christians Want to Know, accessed December 10, 2014, http://www.whatchristianswanttoknow .com/what-is-the-difference-between-faith-and-belief-a-bible-study/.

3. Charles Spurgeon, *The Power of Prayer in a Believer's Life*, comp. and ed. Robert Hall (Lynnwood, WA: Emerald Books, 1993), 157.

4. Bill Hybels and Mark Mittelberg, *Becoming a Contagious Christian* (Grand Rapids, MI: Zondervan, 1996), 41, 42.

CHAPTER TWENTY-THREE

Trials and Team Effort

Who comforts us in all our troubles, so that we can comfort those in any trouble with the comfort we ourselves receive from God.
—2 Corinthians 1:4

I don't know where you live! I don't know where you live!" my father, Marion, said worriedly. I ran out to my car because my mother, Ruthanne, had said, "Here's your chance; make a break for it." My father was in the clingy stage. He followed me from their house out to my car, and I rolled down the window. Then he grasped my open car window as I gave a small explanation of where I lived.

To this, he replied, "I don't know how to get there. Tell me again."

"It's all right, I know where you live, and I will come back."

My father has Alzheimer's disease. We noticed in 1999 that something was wrong, but it was not till 2006 that the general population noticed. People with Alzheimer's are very good at covering with statements such as, "Oh, I forgot," or, "No, the water softener doesn't have to be fixed. That's the way it's supposed to be. It's fine." In reality, they no longer understand the concept why something may need fixing.

Characteristic clues

We were clueless when he quit his job in 1999 when he did not need to. My first inkling that something was not right occurred a few months later when he asked me a question, then thirty minutes later he asked the question again. Gradually, over the next ten years, the time narrowed between when he first asked the question and the second time he asked the same question. It was fascinating and sad to note in 2009 that it took fifteen seconds for him to repeat the same question. We did not need to answer the question anymore because he forgot he asked it.

Did you notice a parallel between my words, "It's all right, I know where you live, and I will come back," and Jesus' words, "Do not let your hearts be troubled. You believe in God; believe also in me. . . . And if I go and prepare a place for you, I will come back" (John 14:1, 3)? These are comforting words for the many horrifying moments my mother, brother, and I have had. You have trials too. And we do not compare trials in order to see who has the larger trial, because everyone in their own trials is trying to cope in their own ways in Christ's strength. So we encourage and pray each other through trials.

My father was always very good at fixing and building anything. He was a church building chairman twice and built two churches. Plus he built sailboats, furniture, a camping tent trailer, and our house. My mother and I roofed and sided while my brother, Mark, and my father did the plumbing, electricity, framing, hanging of cabinets, and so on.

Looking back, my mother would tell you that she had several early clues something was wrong: fixation, driving slowly, and not being able to complete a task. My father would fixate on a task, such as, "I have to get a gasket for the tractor. We need to drive to the store in Woodburn and get a gasket." It was all he could think and talk about; and he drove my mother crazy till they went to get a gasket. Then he did nothing with the gasket, ever. Instead, he drained the hydraulic fluid out of the tractor, which should never ever be done. That was a clue. He was fixated about crown molding for building some library shelving and did fine on the shelving but nailed the crown molding under a window six feet away. My mother was incredulous and asked, "Why did you put the molding under the window?" My father got angry and defended himself that it was correct, which was another sign.

Many interesting things happened when the time between repeated questions narrowed to fifteen seconds. We figured out his brain worked best in the morning, but any new information coming in later started to confuse him. He ate his breakfast, and the conversation was be fine. Next Uncle Dan and Andi came over and talked about Andi going to school in Spain. But when they left, he implored, "Where are my plane tickets? What do I need to pack for my trip?"

People think that those with Alzheimer's forget to do things. However, in the middle stages, it can work like this: you might think he forgot to take a pill; instead, the opposite is true, he thinks he already took it. You start cueing, "You need to go to the bathroom," because you know if she does not, she will forget and have an accident. "No, I don't. I already went." People with Alzheimer's think they have already completed the action. Suddenly, logic and reason do not work all the time. Like leading a horse to water, you can never make it drink. It gets frustrating.

Neurology diagnosis

"I'm so sorry, ma'am. At this stage, there is nothing more we can do. He is in the last stage of the middle stage and the first stage of the last stage." These were the neurologist's words to my mother on May 13, 2009. I have said it before, and I will keep on saying it, "Our God reigns, and He has already won the victory. Our God reigns, and He has already won the victory." Sometimes it does not look like it; however, God continues to involve Himself and intervene in ways that are helpful.

Love Jesus—share Jesus

My father always had enthusiasm for pointing people to Jesus and a love for religious activities. In January 2009, I drove him to the Lake Oswego Community Center for respite care, and he thought he was going to church. While driving, it suddenly occurred to me that time was short, his memory fading, and I did not know his favorite Bible verse. So I asked, "What is your favorite Bible verse?"

He thought for a few moments and said, "I'm not sure; I can't really think of any—oh, 'For God so loved the world' is a good one."

"That's John 3:16," I said and thought, *Why do I always wait until it is too late to ask important questions?*

He continued, "Why? Are we going to have to share it where we are going?"

"No, I was just curious," I responded. Alas, I do not know his favorite verse, but I do know the last one that was on his heart—John 3:16. It is at the heart of salvation: "For God so loved the world that he gave his one and only Son, that whoever believes in him shall not perish but have eternal life."

The care of angels

Ever wonder if angels have to go to the bathroom? This question dawned on me once when I was helping my mother. My mother needed several hours for a break from my father's incessant questioning. I took him on an errand to the mall. Now I do not need to use the bathroom frequently, however, I made the mistake of drinking too much water before I left. We were in Macy's when I realized, *Hmm, I can't leave him by himself. He will forget if I tell him, "I'm going to the bathroom. Stay right here."* He will wander off and get lost or try to purchase something. (This was before we took his wallet away.) Yet, it was here in the mall that I realized, *I can't go to the bathroom, nor can I take him.* If I do not want to leave my charge, how much more does my angel not want to leave me?

Imagine my angel saying, "Oh, right, Diane will wander off, and I won't know where she went. I'm here to protect her, but how can I do that if I'm in the bathroom?" When I returned from mall walking, I related this to my mother who said, "Yes, that is what I have discovered. I have to plan ahead. I scared myself when we went to the symphony our final time. There was a break in the program, so we walked down to the bathroom. He went in the men's, and I went to the women's. I came out, and he did not. I waited and waited, then wondered if he came out and went back to our seats. So I went back to the seats, and he wasn't there. I ran back to the bathroom, and he was just coming out. I might have lost him. It scared me so bad! We can't do that again."

Mother's stories

For a little more than a year, I would drop off my father at respite care on Tuesday and Thursday mornings, and my mom would pick him up in the afternoon. She shared, "If I arrive a little late after most people are gone, it is easier to get him to leave. Otherwise, he literally hangs on to the women helpers and tries not to leave. Reaching the car, I tell him that we are almost out of gas, and we'll get some in West Linn. Why I tell him this, I do not know. Then the misunderstanding in his brain starts up, and he says, 'Something is wrong with the car.'

"I reply, 'No, nothing is wrong with the car. We are just getting gas.'

" 'Something is wrong with the car,' he repeats.

" 'No, nothing is wrong with the car,' I reply and pull over to get gas. I plan to get his watch fixed, then go to the mall to return something at Macy's. By the time we reach Macy's, we are in full scale, 'Something is wrong with the car!' I park at Macy's and turn off the car.

" 'Turn on the car! Turn on the car!' he says. I do this, all the while explaining that nothing is wrong with the car, all we needed was gas.

" 'Try revving it,' he says.

"So I rev it and encourage, 'See it is running smoothly.'

"He jumps out of the car, 'Can you pop the hood?'

" 'No, nothing is wrong with the car,' I reply and do not pop the hood.

At this point, he wants me to get out of the car so he can drive it (like that is going to happen!).

"I think, *Maybe a walk to the mall will help.* No! When we get back to the car, he's still manic. I think, *Maybe going out to eat will help. He can interact with a few people there.*

"As we pull into a parking space at the resturant, there is a woman putting her two children into her car, and he stops to talk to them, which seems to be OK. However, soon the woman finishes strapping the children in and has to come around the car. Marion continues to stand in front of her car door. I say, 'She needs to get into her car; please come with me.' No way. He will not move. He pushes me away. I continue to ask him to let the woman get into her car, all the while trying to get a good grip on him. At this point, he is getting his billfold out of his pocket. I grab his belt and tug. Because he is fumbling with his billfold, this throws him off balance, and he almost brings us both down to the ground. I regain my balance, but he is very angry and curses at me. The woman is wild-eyed now and jumps into her car and backs away.

"He then says, 'I was trying to get twenty dollars for that lady because she was out of gas.'

"After that, I decide we must go straight home after respite care."

Trespassers

At night, Dad frantically paces back and forth through the house, looking for people hiding in the house.

"Would you come back and watch the evening news with me?" Mother inquires. No way. She turns off the news and tries to convince him that no one is in the house. He goes into every room: upstairs, downstairs, all around the house, over and over again, stating, "That man is here. Do I have a gun?"

Replying, "No, you do not have a gun," Mother starts getting ready for bed and then finds him going through her clothes, between the sweaters and shirts. He thinks she has a gun hidden in the house. Finally, at midnight, she gets him into bed, and he falls asleep.

Comic relief moments

One day I arrived to take my parents on a small hike. My mother and I headed out the door with their dog, Annie, and my dad returned to the house. Leaving Annie outside on the porch, my mom and I went back in the house to get my father. Pretty soon Annie pushed the door open and walked in. My dad looked at her and said, "A strange dog just came in the house!" not realizing it was his dog.

The next day he was in the shower and hollered, "Ruthanne, Ruthanne," and she went to the bathroom. He was standing in the bathtub with the shower running and the curtain open and said, "There is water everywhere on the floor!" As the shower was spraying everywhere, she responded, "Well, you could close the shower curtain."

One day I asked my mother, "So what are you going to do today?"

And she replied, "I don't know. Every day is a surprise."

Still caring in 2015

It's 2015 as I recall these "trials" about my father. He and my mother are still hanging in there. Daily my mother sets an excellent example of loving service. My father has many more qualities than just being an example in a chapter called "Trials." When I was a child, he led our devotions and always told me I had a purpose for the Lord. I look forward to his restoration in heaven. He is in the wheelchair stage now and falls to the ground when standing unless someone holds on to him. We also "fall" if we do not hold on to the Lord. I believe God has a plan for your life. Together we need to keep our eyes on heavenly goals, not on the frightful things we call obstacles. If we pray, "Use me," instead of asking "Why me?" then God will bless others through us in wonderful ways. We are encouraged and excited by these words, "Do not let your hearts be troubled. You believe in God; believe also in me. . . . And if I go and prepare a place for you, I will come back" (John 14:1, 3). Our Jesus-help is coming!

Moments of Reflection:

1. Do you have trials God is helping you with right now? Do you know that caring for others also requires caring for yourself? *"Who comforts us in all our troubles, so that we can comfort those in any trouble with the comfort we ourselves receive from God"* (2 Corinthians 1:4).

2. Have you exhausted all the resources available in your area: church, community centers, hospital programs, praying friends? Ask others to do research if you do not have time.

3. If you are not having trials, are you praying for God to show you, with the time and talents you have, who you can minister to? Begin now to pray, "Use me," instead of questioning, "Why me?"

4. Remember to laugh and seek the joy in the present. Help is coming.

CHAPTER TWENTY-FOUR

Prayer That Moves Mountains

"But I know that even now God will give you whatever you ask."
—John 11:22

H i, my name is Linda. I'm from the Florence church, and one of the ladies here has breast cancer. I would like to bring her up for an anointing service with you and Corleen," said Linda. Remembering Linda from a women's retreat and our list of elders, I responded, "Linda, you're an elder. You could save yourself the drive up here [three hours] by gathering a group of ladies in your church and anointing her yourself."

But Linda responded, "No, I really think Kim and I need to come up and see you and Corleen."

"OK, how does next week look for you?" I questioned.

Several days later Corleen and I found a quiet room for anointing Kim. We listened, shared favorite healing verses, prayed, anointed Kim, then sang songs of praise. We encouraged Kim and Linda to keep us in the loop about Kim's progress and promised to continue praying. Quickly switching from the solemnity of the moment, Linda startled me by saying, "We're having a three-church women's retreat in March at the beach. Will you come and be our speaker? Pray about it, and I'll call you."

"That sounds like a wonderful event. All right, I'll pray about it." I thought, *Surely God wants me to go to their retreat. Why wouldn't He?* So I began praying about their retreat and waited for Linda's call.

A turning point

I noticed a need one day several years ago when my husband, Ron, was being negative about marriage—not just a one-day, off-the-cuff comment— but a negative trend. So I called twenty people who I knew would take it seriously and pray if I proclaimed a fast day. They told me which hour they wanted to pray, and the whole day was covered by prayer, hour by hour. I feel very fortunate to know twenty people who will pray for an hour.

A few days later my husband said to me, "I've been thinking and decided that I'm no longer going to associate with Roderick.* He has been a bad influence on me. Two days ago I realized he has been causing me to have a negative perspective about marriage." Inside I did a celebratory *Yahoo*!

A couple of years went by, and long story short, in 2008, I felt impressed about fasting for Ron because God would do something big in his life. Being impulsive at times when God seems to speak, I immediately called my friend Lois and said, "Lois, I'm going to fast from desserts for Ron."

"Are you prepared to do that for life if you have to?" she replied.

I did not have an answer because I was already excited. *Surely God gave me this thought. I wonder what will happen. And, if God is doing something big in someone's life, what is that compared to desserts?* My mind jolted back to the present, and I urged, "Lois, we have to pray because God is going to do something." When you think about it from eternity's vantage point, what is television time or computer time or whatever else you might need to fast from to spend extra time praying for your spouse or your children to come into a relationship with the Lord or whatever the need is? I did not have long to think about it.

Two days later I was in the Christian Supply store to get more anointing oil. As I approached the counter, my hand reached out and grabbed a DVD on display, a movie called *Flywheel.* I drew it up to my eyes to read the subtitle, which read, "In every man's life there's a turning point." Instantly my cell phone rang. Ron sighed, "I'm being let go from work." If I had not just read the subtitle and just given up desserts so that something big would happen in his life, I would have been sad. But I figured that God planned to do something.

Later that day my friend Cheryl heard about Ron and brought over chocolate-chip cookies. Ron ate some and tried to hand me some. I said, "No, you can have them all." He looked at me strangely. But you cannot tell someone, "I'm fasting from desserts, so that God will do something big in your life!"

In my mind, a long time went by, and it seemed like God was way too slow about getting Ron a new job, and I bit my tongue, a lot. He took video training and decided to be a videographer. But finding jobs was difficult.

One March day in 2010, Ron came home from visiting a friend, entered

---

* Roderick is a pseudonym.

the house and pronounced, "I just learned some encouraging news." My ears perked up because I thought maybe he had a job lead. So I replied, "What happened?"

He said, "I was just visiting with Dave, and he showed me this new golf swing that might help my game."

I thought, *Is he kidding? This is not the news I was wishing for.* My mind switched him off as he continued to talk and even did a short demonstration, but I was no longer listening.

The next day he came home with a huge stack of papers and said, "Dave gave me these pages on the new golf swing. It's out of a book he copied on the Internet. Could you take them to Kinko's and copy them for me because Dave needs these back?"

I was now biting my tongue, thinking, *Ron is out of work, and now he wants to spend money on copying these pages about a golf swing.* Sure enough, it cost twenty-seven dollars to copy all of those pages. I brought them home and handed the stack to him still biting my tongue. He grasped the stack and immediately started reading the pages, but he said aloud, "And all this in answer to a prayer."

"What?" I replied and turned back around.

He jumped up and started to demonstrate, sharing, "I used to hold the club like this, but Dave said the book says this is better. See the difference?"

Blinking my eyes in wonder at his definition of answered prayer, I asked, "How is this an answer to your prayer?"

Ron responded, "Three days ago I was so discouraged that I prayed to God for encouragement, and this is how He encouraged me!"

God always has a plan

We think we know how God should answer our prayers for someone else, but God answers them according to His plan. "But I know that even now God will give you whatever you ask" (John 11:22). And Matthew 21:22 says, "If you believe, you will receive whatever you ask for in prayer." Trouble is, it doesn't say *when*!

A long time went by, and one morning I went into the living room. Ron was reading on the couch, and I sat in a chair behind him. I decided not to ask him if he wanted me to read him something from the Bible for devotions, because the day before he did not. As I looked at him and then my Bible, my eyes fell on an encouraging promise. *What a blessing, surely now God is up to something big. I don't have to do anything,* I thought.

That very day my friend Lois called Ron and shared that Derek Morris was having meetings at her Vancouver church. She thought the church was videoing this, and Ron should check it out. So he went and met Todd Gessele at the meeting. Todd asked him if he wanted to go with the Oregon Adventist Men's Chorus (OAMC) on a mission trip to Romania. It was such an out-of-the-blue request that he decided it was a "God thing," and he went and has been videoing the OAMC ever since, which has led to other jobs.

Do you get excited about how God works? He has timing down to a science!

Three-church women's retreat

"What did God tell you about coming to our retreat?" Linda asked.

"Well, He didn't say No, so I would be delighted to come," I replied.

Time flew by as we shared and covered the retreat in prayer. We decided I needed to give my testimony in their first meeting and then other topics on Sabbath and Sunday.

That first weekend of March 2007 was a beautiful weekend for the Oregon coast, and I thoroughly enjoyed getting to know the ladies, sharing what God has done in my life and how we all can share the knowledge God gives us. "Being confident of this, that he who began a good work in you will carry it on to completion until the day of Christ Jesus" (Philippians 1:6).

I urged, "Many Reformers before us have shared what God showed them. William Tyndale is one that comes to mind. He lived in the sixteenth century and was a brilliant scholar of that age and a teacher at Oxford. He didn't have a big flowery title like president of the college. He was just a teacher. He shared that the glory of God is found in devotion, faith, and service and not in one's title, power, or wealth. He emphasized that one's own interpretation of the Bible is a better guide for moral living and that sacraments are not the way to salvation. John Wycliffe taught that God's forgiveness cannot be bought by indulgences and wanted the church to prove its position with Scripture. He preached that the only true authority is the Word of God. Wycliffe was a great man of faith and prayer. It was his study of Scripture that set him apart."

Between the meetings, I found out that Linda is a woman of prayer and biblical knowledge as she shared her heart, and we prayed for the ladies and the next meeting.

Over the years, I continued to be invited to speak at the Florence retreat and church and grew to love the ladies of Florence. In between those times, Linda and I would meet in places such as Lincoln City and eastern Oregon for a few days of prayer, hiking, and fellowship, and we became great friends.

You may remember the mission trip in Madras; it was there that Linda declared to everyone, "This is a mission trip that I can go on because I don't fly!" In private, she shared later, "Not until we go to heaven will I go up in the clouds." I asked a few questions, but she did not budge about flying. At that time, I started praying about it in my personal prayers.

A year and a month went by, and on July 29, 2009, Linda and I met in Lincoln City for prayers and fellowship. While we were in Lincoln City, I asked Linda, "Would you and your husband, George, like to go with Ron and me to Arizona for fun?" Long story short, she wavered, at first saying yes, then two days later, saying no and, with finality, "God needs to give me the sign I am asking for, or I'm not flying." I love Arizona and wanted Linda to enjoy it, too, so this was a serious issue for me.

Fasting to overcome strongholds

An hour later I felt impressed to fast over this issue. So I started scanning my Bible and looking at the books on my shelf, and I noticed one title, *Fasting for Spiritual Breakthrough* by Elmer Towns. I opened it and chose the chapter on Ezra because Ezra fasted for a specific problem. In fact, the interesting thing was, "Ezra implemented old-fashioned prayerwalking by bringing the people face to face with their problem—he brought them to the banks of the river before launching out into the wilderness. 'Beside the Ahava River, I asked the people to go without eating and to pray.' "[1]

Placing the book down, I quickly grabbed the phone, "Linda, I feel impressed to fast. I have this book that says Ezra brought people to the location of the problem. Maybe you should go to the airport, and I'll go to an airport."

"We have one in Florence," she affirmed.

"When can you go?" I asked.

"Tuesday would work," she responded.

"Then Tuesday it is, and we can pray and fast together. Do you mind if I ask Lois to pray also?"

"Sure, that's fine," she said.

Inside I was jumping up and down that surely God would do something. Tuesday arrived, my eyes popped open, and I started praying, "Lord, please protect and guide this airport project, and break down the walls of spiritual oppression over flying for Linda." An unexpected thought came to my mind, *"Take your black coat to give away."*

What? Today? I guess I can work that in. I had heard that a lady lost her coat. Since I was fasting, I drank a little juice, obediently grabbed the coat, and called her.

"Yes, please drop by," she affirmed. "I want to see your coat; mine was stolen last week."

This seemed to be unusual timing, but she loved the coat. "Are you going to work? You came out of your way if you are," she asked.

"No, I'm going to the airport to pray," I shared. She looked at me funny, so I said, "I'm going to pray for someone who has a fear of flying."

She said, "Then pray for me also."

"All right, and we can have a little prayer right now in person," I agreed and sent up a prayer.

At the airport, I prayed for a while, claimed some verses, then called Lois to pray with me.

Scriptures for strongholds

These are some verses I claimed:

- Ezra 8:21–23: "There, by the Ahava Canal, I proclaimed a fast, so that we might humble ourselves before our God and ask him for a safe journey for us and our children, with all our possessions. I was ashamed to ask the king for soldiers and horsemen to protect us from enemies on the road, because we had told the king, 'The gracious hand of our God is on everyone who looks to him, but his great anger is against all who forsake him.' So we fasted and petitioned our God about this, and he answered our prayer."
- Psalm 94:19: "When anxiety was great within me, your consolation brought me joy."
- Psalm 94:22: "But the LORD has become my fortress, and my God the rock in whom I take refuge."

Lois prayed and claimed these verses:

- Psalm 138:8: "The LORD will fulfill his purpose for [Linda]; your steadfast love, O LORD, endures forever. Do not forsake the work of your hands" (ESV).

- Philippians 2:13: "For it is God who works in you to will and to act in order to fulfull his good purpose."
- Philippians 4:6, 7: "Do not be anxious about anything, but in every situation, by prayer and petition, with thanksgiving, present your requests to God. And the peace of God, which transcends all understanding, will guard your hearts and your minds in Christ Jesus."

"Lord, please remove any spiritual oppression from Linda. Please help my friend and the coat lady who are afraid." I spent at least an hour in prayer, partly with Lois, then by myself. I finally ended with these thoughts and with my hand up for emphasis, "Lord, I don't know what is going to happen as a result of these prayers. But I am claiming that we at least poked holes in this flying stronghold, and it will come down!"

Arriving at work later, my coworker, Tracy, came by and asked, "Would you be able to take my worship for August 17? I'm going to be gone." It was as if God was confirming, "I like what you did at the airport. Here's a blessing for you!" Prayer really does move mountains.

Moments of Reflection:

1. If you have not felt covered by prayer in a special way, then gather a few friends or people from church, open the Scriptures, share requests, and pray for each other.

2. Do you wish for something big to happen? Ponder the issue, find a location, re-read Ezra 8 or the book of Ezra, gather a few more scriptures, and go pray. Do not forget your journal, and continue to praise and pray till you see a response or feel like God has brought closure.

---

1. Elmer Towns, *Fasting for Spiritual Breakthrough* (Ventura, CA: Regal Books, 1996), 49.

CHAPTER TWENTY-FIVE

Prayer That Conquers the Unknown

If I ascend into heaven, You are there; If I make my bed in hell,
behold, You are there. If I take the wings of the morning,
and dwell in the uttermost parts of the sea, even there
Your hand shall lead me, and Your right hand shall hold me.
—Psalm 139:8–10, NKJV

I have a little packet of Taco Bell sauce hanging on the wall above my computer, daily reminding me, "If you never do, you'll never know." On Thursday, October 28, 2010, God said to me, *"Fast three days next week, Monday, Tuesday, and Wednesday."* No further instructions came; just that phrase. I was left to wonder what God was up to; but with the urge to fast for three days, it had to be something big. Sabbath arrived, and Linda happened to be visiting my church. Dan Serns was preaching because he was leading an evangelistic series the next week. Dan was the former North Pacific Union Conference Ministerial director who organized the Bolivian mission trip that I went on in 2006. He was now the pastor at the Richardson Seventh-day Adventist Church in Texas. As Linda and I shook his hand after his sermon that day, he said to me, "How's the world evangelist?"

I responded, "Funny you should say that, *evangelist* is my password at work."

He asked, "So where are you going next?"

"I don't have anything lined up," I shared.

"We are organizing a trip to the Dominican Republic. My daughter, Danesa, chose the location. Why don't you both come and be a team?" he said, looking at Linda also.

Linda laughed and said, "I don't fly," then looked at me as if to say, *Don't even think about it.*

I did not have to say anything because God's words came back to my mind, *"Fast three days next week, Monday, Tuesday, and Wednesday,"* and I knew she was going.

Monday was my first day of fasting. That day I heard at the office they were talking about my position. A few days later on November 11, 2010, I was downsized at the office. It is interesting that the evil one is so frightened by fasting that he will do anything to stop it. Jobs that people bestow on you will come and go, nevertheless, God's open position in the harvest field continues till He comes.

On Tuesday and Wednesday, November 2 and 3, were also spent in fasting and prayer. On Thursday morning, Linda called me and sounded all excited and shared, "God woke me up at 3:00 A.M. in the morning, and I couldn't go back to sleep! Right handy next to the bed there was a copy of Acts of the Apostles. I opened it and noticed it was all about Paul's journeys, Paul's travels. He went here, then he went there. I closed it and opened the Bible and looked at the maps in the back, and God's voice came to me, *'If Paul had had a plane, where would he have gone?'* And then God's voice came to me again, *'You need to go and tell what great things I have done for you.'"*

"Linda, this is huge! I'm so glad you are going!" I said excitedly.

Then her next words were, "How am I going to pay for this?"

"Are you kidding?" I replied, "Everyone in your church and community knows you don't fly. They will be lining up to pay money to see you fly!"

"Maybe I'll mention at our board meeting that I am going to the Dominican Republic on a mission trip," she ventured. A week later she called to say, "Over the last week, there was a little turmoil. I am still not hot on wanting to get on a plane. One restless night I couldn't relax and sat down on the couch next to George and opened my Bible and opened to Psalms, and my eyes fell on chapter 139. I started with verse 5 and read through verse 11 and then said, 'George, this is unbelievable! Listen!'

"You have hedged me behind and before,
And laid Your hand upon me.
Such knowledge is too wonderful for me;
It is high, I cannot attain it.

"Where can I go from Your Spirit?
Or where can I flee from Your presence?
If I ascend into heaven, You are there;
If I make my bed in hell, behold, You are there.

If I take the wings of the morning,
And dwell in the uttermost parts of the sea,
Even there Your hand shall lead me,
And Your right hand shall hold me.
If I say, 'Surely the darkness shall fall on me,'
Even the night shall be light about me" (NKJV).

After reading me this, Linda continued, "A few days later while driving home from Eugene, Corleen called me and said, 'I feel God has given me verses for you.' She also read Psalm 139:5–11. Especially emphasizing verse 9, saying, 'You will be flying to the other side of the sea.' Can you believe that? That was when I began to have greater peace of mind about the airplane trip. As if God was saying, *I will be on the flight with you.*'"

She phoned me again after the next board meeting. Linda said, "They were stunned, and then someone shared, 'This is truly from God. We're going to mention your trip at church and your need for funds.' On my behalf, Todd, a board member, stood up in church and received stunned silence when he said, 'How many of you would pay money to see Linda get on an airplane?' They all raised their hands, and my way has been paid. Can you believe it?"

"Yes, I can believe it. That's great!" I said.

Prayer walking

The previous year, on Thursday, September 16, 2010, I was in Florence, Oregon, helping Linda's church with a ministry event in a local park. On our route, we kept driving by an area that the Lord indicated to us was in need of prayer. We decided to prayer walk around the area later in the afternoon. A few hours later, as we were leaving the local park, it started to rain, and I thought, *Oh, great. Now it is raining, and we still should prayer walk that area.* We drove up, this time in two cars, and parked. Rain was falling at an angle, and because it was a huge block to go around, I said, "Why don't we just go once around and then six more another day?" We went around once praying and claiming scriptures.

Linda urged, "Let's go once more." On the second time, as we reached within eyeshot of the front door of one building, two twenty-something girls appeared and started shouting at us.

One of them shouted, "What is your name? What is your name?"

To which, Linda replied, "My name is Linda. What is yours?"

The woman said, "Samantha."

"Why don't you walk with us?" Linda beckoned.

Samantha said very loudly and in what seemed to be an unusual tone, "*No!*"

Since we were finished walking, we turned and got in our cars. Linda's was in front of mine. As she drove away, I noticed that it was dry where her car had been and wet all around it.

The Lord said to me, *"You left an impression."*

That evening, as we were in our hotel room, Linda suddenly stated, "You know those girls said, 'What is your name?' "

The moment Linda mentioned this I got chills and felt a strange presence.

I stood bolt upright and said, "That's it!" I walked intentionally toward my Bible, opened it to Matthew 4:10, "Away from me, Satan! For it is written: 'Worship the Lord your God, and serve him only.' " And the presence left. Linda gave voice to her thoughts, "I had chills just now. Those girls were demons or had demons speaking through them. Something happened in that area this evening."

Walking by faith, not by sight

Linda has rosacea in her eyes, which means her eyes have trouble in bright light and heat. Plus, she needs glasses for distance. More than once through the years she has mentioned she would like to ditch her glasses. A couple of months before our trip, she mentioned, "I'm praying for cool weather for my eyes for the Dominican Republic. However, it will be nice to walk on a warm, sunny beach. Oregon beaches are cold." I was looking forward to warmth as well. It was January 22, and we were at her church's retreat, a cold but lovely spot in Eagle Crest.

Conquering the unknown

My friend Georgia Shaffer, in her book *A Gift of Mourning Glories*, describes the Israelites and their fear to enter the Promised Land, saying,

> Their cowardly attitude and refusal to fight infuriated God and earned them another forty years of desert travel. . . .
>
> Conquering unknown territory becomes necessary if we are to move beyond our losses to a new life. We need to take the risk, face our fears, and do what terrifies us. If we don't, we may find ourselves wandering around in the desert for another forty years.[1]

My *Life Application Study Bible* comments about Nehemiah, "We frequently underestimate people and don't challenge them with our dreams for God's work in the world. When God plants an idea in your mind to accomplish something for him, share it with others and trust the Holy Spirit to impress them with similar thoughts. Don't regard yourself as the only one through whom God is working. . . . When you encourage and inspire others, you put teamwork into action to accomplish God's goals."[2] Esther faced her fear and did what was terrifying, but she did it with the help of many others who were fasting at the same time.

Dominican Republic

Sometimes life is not a picnic, but it can still be a blessing.

"This is not enjoyable. Is there always this much turbulence when you fly?" Linda asked about forty-five minutes into our overnight flight to Atlanta, on the way to the Dominican Republic, on March 10, 2011. It did seem odd that her first flight would be so bumpy. Thankfully, the second leg over the mesmerizingly beautiful Atlantic Ocean was smooth.

"Wasn't someone coming to meet us? We've been waiting here for a while," Linda questioned as we stood at the curb after going through customs.

"I don't know. In third world countries, one never knows what will happen. I'm just praying and watching," I responded.

"It doesn't look like anyone knows we're here. How long are you going to pray before you do something?" Linda asked thirty minutes later.

"I'm not sure what there is to do. Oh, wait. I just remembered; I wrote someone's number on a three-by-five card," I replied and sorted through some paperwork.

"Excuse me," I said, motioning to some official-looking person, "may I use your phone?"

A tall, stocky fellow held out his phone to me.

"Well, you will need to dial this number for me," I said and waited to grab the phone but held out my phone number. He called and gave it back to me. "Bueno," someone said but seemed to understand my limited Spanish. "I call ride for you," the person said and hung up.

Five minutes later a small boy walked toward us, holding a sign with our names on it. Linda was so excited, she hugged him.

At the hotel, our young roommate Lillian, who was twenty-three, said upon meeting us, "Oh, I figured you guys were my age, but you're older." Later Linda and I had a good laugh.

During the first group meeting, when asked about why we came, Linda had quite the testimony, "Only God could get me on a plane. I'll be interested to see what all He has in store for this trip." We did not have long to wait.

Our hotel looked like a compound with high walls but was an improvement over the surroundings. Linda said, "We are in a hotel, but this is camping." One window would not shut, letting mosquitoes and smoky air in, and ash pieces would also float in from the nearby sugar plant. However, the best part was the ocean right across the street, so, of course, I wanted to walk there. While wading in the water, I noticed people kept staring at us, and no one else was in the water. Back at the hotel we were told, "You were wading where the sewage drains from the city into the ocean." Yikes, what a thought! We did not expect that news!

Our church

The next day we went on visitations and then to our church for the meeting. "How far is it to our church?" I asked someone.

"It's just over one kilometer," the person said.

A better description would be this, "After you slow down for all the stray dogs, motorcycles, food vendor carts, horses pulling carts, intersections without stop signs, and accident scenes, it takes about twenty minutes." Our church people were very proud because they had a brand-new church, and it was lovely. It was only missing one thing—a bathroom.

Linda was a little dismayed that our interpreter did not speak enough English. "I came all this way, and now I'm so sad that the people can't understand all that I am saying," she lamented to me. We started praying about it. On Friday night, as Linda was lying on her bed feeling anxious about what would happen the next morning when she tried to share her testimony, she immediately remembered God had told her to go and tell what great things He had done for her. When that thought came to her, she presented her request to God for the ability to be able to share so the people would understand. On Sabbath morning, God did something special as Linda shared her testimony. She said later, "It was as if the Holy Spirit was speaking through the interpreter. All of my words he suddenly seemed to clearly understand, and I looked out at the people and there were smiles and tears in the appropriate places like they understood. We read in the book of Acts about the gift of tongues, and I felt that our interpreter received the gift of interpretation, so that the people could hear what great things God had done in my life, because that is why He sent me here."

Confirmation

A couple of days later we received this e-mail from our friend Tami, "We have enjoyed your e-mails so much it has been the center of our worship every evening—we read your e-mail and then have prayer for your meetings and visitations—it is like a mission story where we actually know the missionaries. How are you doing? I wanted to let you know that Sabbath morning I suddenly woke up at 5:00 A.M. and the Lord said, *'Pray for Linda,'* so I immediately started praying for you both and then wished later I could actually talk to you. . . . Most importantly, how are the meetings going?" Linda and I looked at each other, and I said, "That is incredible! God woke up Tami to pray, so that your testimony could be understood."

"Locked down" for prayer

One day Linda and I "locked" ourselves in our room. When we arrived at the hotel, they handed us a key and said, "Don't lose it, it is the only one we have." And I thought, *Surely they have more than one.* One time our other roomie had the key, and we could not find her. Finally, the desk clerk tracked down a security guard with the one master key. So here we were again without a key. The door would lock behind us when we closed it with no way to unlock it. Thus, we could not leave our room. As we were searching for the key, the words we said to Dustin, our mission team leader, came back to me, "We will be praying in our room today instead of doing visitations."

As if God were ensuring prayer would happen, He "locked" us in.

"Linda, I think God wants us to pray about something," I suggested. We had quality prayer time, and, of course, Linda found our key after that. We walked out of the room, and as we walked, Linda noticed her vision seemed blurry with her glasses. We reached the tiny fifth floor lobby's picture window, which overlooked the beautiful terrain. Then as if God was so excited that we took extra time for prayer, we noticed a miracle. Linda stopped by the window and said, "I want to try something." She took off her glasses.

"No way!" she said.

"What?" I asked.

She pushed her glasses up and down before her eyes.

"God healed my eyes! I can see perfectly without my glasses!"

We became certain that God gave Linda a gift for stepping out in faith on a mission trip. The heat no longer bothered her eyes, and she has never worn glasses for distance since. Later that night she was reviewing her notes, and she thought, *I still have to wear my glasses to read. God, if You were going to heal my eyes, why didn't You heal them all the way?*

God replied, *"Because you are now farsighted."* This made her think that this related to the fact that she stretched herself by going on the plane. And it is a good reminder that God wants us to be farsighted, to go beyond what we are capable.

A few nights later and after some visitations with the locals, we were assigned a child that looked to be about the age of six. This child was to walk us through the night streets to a church member's house who would take us to the meeting. We started walking with no streetlights, so it was very dim light. I thought, *Is this safe? If we lose sight of this small child, we are here in the dark where we don't know any place or anyone. Lord, please help us.*

Linda interrupted my thoughts, "Diane, some guys are yelling at us. Start praying!" We heard, "Americana! Americana!"

"Diane, you have a computer and a bag full of stuff; keep praying," she urged. I was praying and did not turn around but kept focused on the small child. Linda said, "They're running at us!" Then she said, "Hey, where did they go? They disappeared just like that." God stepped in, and we soon arrived safely at our destination.

Perspective

In an e-mail home, I conveyed, "We can share things, like Linda and I have one more mosquito bite each, and the shower is now cold again. That the locals say we are in the poorest part of the Dominican Republic. That the power went out at one of our sites. That every morning at 6 A.M. the tsunami warning system sounds, and you can hear it for miles. But does this really matter in the big picture?

"Linda says, 'We will get on a plane and leave for a home and country that has many amenities, but these people will remain and struggle to survive. It makes me wonder what we should be doing with the things that God has blessed us with. Thank the Lord for blessing America because He really has.'

"The people we reach for the Lord are the most important job we have in this life. Remember the older lady that wanted me just to pray. Last night she came up to me at the beginning of the meeting. She pointed at her hip and said in Spanish she was in pain and wanted prayer. I asked, *'Es muy mala?'* (Is it very bad?)

" *'Sí,'* she responded.

"I grabbed her hands and prayed in Spanish then English and finished in Spanish, which made her think I know more Spanish than I do. I grabbed a Spanish Bible, opened it up to Números (Numbers) 6:24–26, and handed it to her, pointing at the text.

"She expressed, *'No puedo leer'* (I can't read). I pulled it back and read in Spanish and watched as her expression changed to one of peace. If only we could do this for every person on earth. These are blessed words from God,

" ' " 'The LORD bless you
     and keep you;
   the LORD make his face shine on you
     and be gracious to you;
   the LORD turn his face toward you
     and give you peace' " ' " (Numbers 6:24–26).

Another e-mail home

"We have heard many wonderful testimonies of what God is doing here in the lives of the people from other sites as well as ours. This morning I slept past the tsunami warning (that's a first!), but let us not sleep past God's warnings. It is wonderful to be part of the end-time Revelation 14 message. Little did we know, after the first tsunami warning that we had, that there was a real, unimaginable tsunami that hit Japan on March 11 the day after we arrived. Linda's son had to flee their city of Florence (on the Oregon coast). This reminded us of the verses in Revelation 7:1 and 3 that describe the four winds that are being let loose in God's timing: 'After this I saw four angels standing at the four corners of the earth, holding back the four winds of the earth to prevent any wind from blowing on the land or on the sea or on any tree. . . . "Do not harm the land or the sea or the trees until we put a seal on the foreheads of the servants of our God." '

"So what we saw in Japan is only a glimpse of what will take place in the future, and we need to allow God to use us to give this warning message to the world. That includes you also. 'We are therefore Christ's ambassadors, as though God were making his appeal through us' (2 Corinthians 5:20). May God guide and bless you as you share today. Blessings, Diane."

The mission continues till Jesus comes

Several months after our mission trip, it was June 18, 2011, and I was at home reading in Psalms when I looked down at the study notes that read, "The brevity of life is a theme throughout the books of Psalms, Proverbs, and Ecclesiastes." "Life is short no matter how long we live. If we have something important we want to do, we must not put it off for a better day. Ask yourself, If I had only six months to live, what would I do?"[3] It felt like God really was asking me the question and expecting an answer. So I pronounced, "I would do an evangelistic series again."

"Well, then, what are you waiting for?" He seemed to say.

I prayed, picked up the phone, and called Corleen to mention what just happened, and then added, "You know, I would really like to go to Arizona. Don't you have a friend that lives there?"

"Yes," she replied.

"What is the name of his church? Maybe that's a place to start." We prayed and I called the church pastor where her friend attended. Long story short and many twists and turns later, Linda and I put on a two-week cooking school in Sierra Vista, Arizona, in October 2012.

God showed me that sharing about my passion for eating healthfully is also mission work. Stretch yourself because God wants you to be farsighted for Him. What is God calling you to do? "If you never do, you'll never know." Once you have overcome a stronghold with God, you will never be willing to let one stand in your way again.

Moments of Reflection:

1. How does it make you feel that God chose you, loves you, and calls you His friend?

2. How does it make you feel that God entrusts you with a mission for others for His kingdom?

3. Do you have a verse that describes your identity in Christ?

4. What's your response to God's words in Judges 3:28, "Follow me"?

---

1. Georgia Shaffer, *A Gift of Mourning Glories* (Ann Arbor, MI: Vine Books, 2000), 136.
2. *Life Application Study Bible: New Living Translation,* 745.
3. Ibid., 864.